OLD SCHOOL

OLD SCHOOL

Life in the Sane Lane

Bill O'Reilly
and Bruce Feirstein

Henry Holt and Company
New York

Henry Holt and Company
Publishers since 1866
175 Fifth Avenue
New York, New York 10010
www.henryholt.com

Henry Holt® and ® are registered trademarks of
Macmillan Publishing Group, LLC.

Library of Congress Cataloging-in-Publication Data is available.

ISBN: 9781250135797

Our books may be purchased in bulk for promotional, educational, or
business use. Please contact your local bookseller or the Macmillan
Corporate and Premium Sales Department at (800) 221-7945, extension 5442,
or by e-mail at MacmillanSpecialMarkets@macmillan.com.

First Edition 2017

Designed by Meryl Sussman Levavi

Printed in the United States of America

1   3   5   7   9   10   8   6   4   2

BVG

Contents

Greetings from
1973

Man, it was a long, hot ride. It was June, and O'Reilly had just finished up his second year of teaching English and history at Pace High School, in Opa-locka, Florida, just north of Miami. Please don't consider vacationing there. It's known as the crack capital of Dade County. No beaches, plenty of home invasions.

Teaching working-class kids suited me well. I liked most of my pupils and tried to steer the kids toward success. The student body was a fascinating mixture of Cuban Americans, whites, and a few African Americans.

I used discipline and honesty in the classroom, forcing the urchins to do their assignments and pointing out to the slackers that if they avoided college, things could get very dicey in the real world.

One time, I put on a slide show of ghetto life to get my point across, but, really, all these kids had to do was look out the window.

In 1973, I was twenty-four years old and had not really developed a consistent philosophy of life. But I was raised in a traditional Irish-Catholic home and embraced the decency found in it.

In history classes, I promoted traditional thought in a year when the U.S. government was falling part. President Richard Nixon would be gone in two months, the victim of his own dishonesty. Daily, the press barbecued him over the Watergate mess, and the entire two-year-long tragedy fascinated me.

So, I decided to do something about it. I applied to and was accepted at Boston University's broadcast journalism master's degree program. Coincidentally, my mother had graduated from BU three decades before, studying physical therapy.

The summer ride from South Florida to the Commonwealth of Massachusetts is hot. Not tepid, but torrid. The dead bugs on my windshield loved it, right up until they became oatmeal.

My old car was not air-conditioned. Sweat poured off me like Albert Brooks in *Broadcast News* as I zoomed past Jacksonville, Savannah, a tourist trap called South of the Border, Richmond, and on up into the Northeast. I don't remember whining about the incessant heat, and to this day, folks who constantly tell the world about their personal temperature situation annoy me.

Stop. Life is not climate-controlled, people. Accept it. Don't be a Snowflake, a condition we will soon describe.

Little did I know that my eighteen-month tenure at Boston U would not only lay the groundwork for my journalism career, but would also begin my new life in another school: Old School.

In the following pages, that Old School journey will be laid out with the help of a fellow Old School traveler. I met Bruce Feirstein at BU, and there the Old School legend was made.

As the Hollies once warbled, "The road is long / with many a winding turn."

Feirstein and I are glad you're along for the ride. It's air-conditioned this time.

Preschool

Take Your Seat

My father, Bill O'Reilly Sr., bought his pants through the mail. Toward the end of his life, retired and always looking to save a few bucks, he'd order polyester trousers from a catalog. I think the price was $29.95.

$32.50 in today's dollars.

Problem was the pants were always too short, as my dad was six foot three. But he didn't care. Children of the Great Depression, Old School people who survived economic Armageddon, had strict priorities: if you could save a dollar, you saved a dollar.

One day, I blew in to visit my folks from somewhere and encountered my father wearing mustard-colored pants held up by red suspenders. After the initial greeting, this back-and-forth took place:

"Dad, your pants are too short."

"Who are you, Oleg Cassini now?"*

"And what color is that?"

"They're yellow. Do you have astigmatism?"

"Come on, Dad, this is not a good presentation. You don't leave the house wearing those things, do you?"

My father paused, giving me a look. He knew I was jazzing him, but his sense of humor overrode any offense.

"Don't remember you checking out my wardrobe when I was paying for your college."

"Yeah, but you didn't look like one of the Village People back then."

My father actually laughed and walked into the kitchen. He wore those pants for years.

We are all products of our upbringing, and it used to be that Old School philosophy, which we'll define throughout this book, ruled, at least in working-class homes throughout the country.

No longer.

Now there is an ongoing battle between traditional Americans and those who want a kinder, gentler landscape full of "conversations" and group hugs, folks who believe that life must be fair and that, if it is not, there has to be a "safe space" available where they can cry things out.

I cringe when I see this kind of stuff and immediately time-travel back to my Levittown, New York, neighborhood in the 1960s, where my pal Clement would have definitely said, "Hey, I've got your safe space *right here!*"

A physical flourish would have accompanied Clem's remark.

The bedrock truth is that life is hard, especially if you have to

---

* An American playboy fashion designer of Russian descent who created First Lady Jackie Kennedy's pillbox hat.

compete for prosperity. Rather than major in whining, Old School folks tough it out, developing skills to overcome the inevitable obstacles every human being faces.

We all know Snowflakes: the people who blame everyone else for their failures, who look to others to solve their problems, who are sooooo sensitive to every slight.

Boring. And stupid. Don't be that person. Absorb the lessons we are about to impart.

When I looked around for someone with whom to write this book, my friend Bruce Feirstein emerged as the perfect choice. Biggest advantage: he is not like me.

Diplomatic and somewhat cerebral, Feirstein had huge early career success with a book called *Real Men Don't Eat Quiche*, which was actually a humorous warning about Snowflake culture long before it existed. Then Bruce went on to write Hollywood scripts along with articles for the *Wall Street Journal* and *Vanity Fair*, among others. He lives in Los Angeles, so he's enmeshed in Snowflake culture; it affects him every day.

While I embrace an East Coast swagger, Feirstein does not immediately alienate half the universe as I have a tendency to do, but we are both Old School guys, as you will soon see. However, we take different buses to the school, which makes things interesting.

I will concede that America will never go back to the Old School curriculum that many Baby Boomers experienced. Not gonna happen with so many lawyers running wild.

Here's what I'm talking about.

If I'd worn a bicycle helmet when I was a kid, I would have been mocked beyond belief, and the helmet would immediately have been taken off my head and placed somewhere far away. Maybe Rhode Island.

If my mom had defended me after a kid-on-kid altercation, I could never have left the house again.

If my dad had yelled at the Little League coach, air might have left the tires of our family car.

If I'd borrowed money from another kid to buy a Three Musketeers and didn't pay it back, no one would have played with me.

If a kid kicked someone in a fight, he was blacklisted. Only fists, and no hitting when someone was down.

If a girl cursed, silence ensued. For a long time. And boys *never* bothered girls because of the "Brother and His Large Friends" rule.

When Feirstein and I were growing up, Mom and Dad were not told everything. In fact, they were told nothing unless the police or fire department arrived at the house.

Most parents seemed to like it that way.

And then there was prevailing wisdom.

Anybody who sold drugs in the neighborhood was scum, the lowest. Irredeemable.

Kids who were different were generally okay, unless they flaunted the situation. There was some bullying, but my crew didn't like it, and sometimes confronted it.

However, there was a kid nicknamed Eggy who got hammered. One day, his father told my father about it. Later, I was called into the living room—never a good thing.

"Why are you bothering Eddie? You're calling him 'Eggy.' Why?"

"He's a dope."

"And you're a genius?"

I could see this wasn't heading in a good direction.

"Uh, we don't like him."

"Why?"

"I don't know."

"And you're calling him a dope? No more. Don't bother the kid anymore. Got it? And tell your dim pals to knock it off, too."

"Okay."

So, we knocked it off. My Old School father was not to be trifled with.

"How mad was he?" one of my moronic friends asked.

"One step away from pain," I answered.

So "Eddie" replaced "Eggy" in a classic case of Old School justice.

It is not Old School to live in the past, but remembering how things were as opposed to how things are now is a required course.

So, let's get started.

Introducing
the Old School
Curriculum

For Baby Boomers and the Greatest Generation, the changes in America over the past seventy years have been staggering.

Just imagine Gen. George Patton on Snapchat. Or how about James Dean pulling a Bruce Jenner? The world is evolving. And soon there will be a final showdown. The two teams: Old School versus Snowflakes.

Which team are you on?

Are You Old School, or Are You a Snowflake?

A Pop Quiz

If you're unsure of exactly where you stand in the Old School curriculum, the following questions may help clarify things:

1) Do you still have a landline telephone?
    a) Yes. b) No. c) What's a landline?

2) Do you still balance your checking account every month?
    a) Yes. b) No. c) I don't know because my parents are still paying for everything.

3) If someone wishes you "Merry Christmas," what's your immediate response?
    a) Return the greeting, adding "And a Happy New Year."
    b) Call the ACLU or Human Resources to launch a formal complaint that it's an exclusionary and divisive micro-aggression that can only be remedied with either the greeter being fired or a multimillion-dollar legal settlement for your pain and suffering.

4) Which best reflects your view on dealing with terrorists?
    a) "There is only one 'retirement plan' for terrorists" (U.S. secretary of defense and former U.S. Marine general James "Mad Dog" Mattis). b) "Our most effective response to terror and to hatred is compassion, it's unity, and it's love" (former U.S. attorney general Loretta Lynch).

5) If you happen upon a raging warehouse fire late at night, do you:
    a) Hope the firefighters are safe and express concern for the people who work there during the day. b) Get out of your car and take a selfie with the fire in the background?

If you *are* Old School, the answers should be obvious. Otherwise, read on.

* * *

Old School is now in session. The lesson plan is really quite easy.

Did you get up this morning knowing there are mountains to climb, and deciding that somehow you are going to climb them?

Or did you wake up whining about safe spaces and trigger warnings ("Caution: The following may be offensive")? Are you one of those millions of people who actively look for something to get outraged about, every single day, so you can fire off a tweet defending your exquisitely precious sensibilities?

In essence, Snowflakes are folks who go where the prevailing winds take them, often melting down when things get hot.

There is no middle ground here. You have to choose. This book will be your guide—are you Old School or will you melt in August?

Some hints.

That cashier at Home Depot putting herself through college ringing up Sheetrock? Old School.

Kanye West forever mouthing off, portraying himself as a victim? Snowflake.

To be honest, the authors of this book are Old School guys who met at Boston University in 1974. Then, like now, college campuses were in an uproar. It was the era of Richard Nixon, the Watergate break-in, the women's movement, and the war in Vietnam. Faith in America and the U.S. government was not exactly at an all-time high. And on college campuses across America, Students for a Democratic Society staged sit-ins and protests, demanding an end to the war, an end to the draft, and an end to military recruiters and the ROTC. It was a time of social transition that still reverberates today.

At the time, the authors of this book regularly traded jibes over these issues in Boston University's newspaper, *Daily Free Press.*

And while we may not always agree on things, we shared something that became the basis for a lifetime friendship: both of us were working-class guys without money or social connections. By working hard and persevering, we eventually succeeded in the marketplace, shocking many who knew us. One of the reasons we succeeded—something neither of us knew at the time—was that we were ferociously hard workers. We painted houses in the summer to pay for school. Unlike Bernie Sanders, we didn't expect anybody else to pay for our higher education. That's the difference between the Snowflake view of the world, and Old School.

There is not one single definition, or one single thing that makes someone Old School. But as classic Old School guy Rod Serling* might have said, there are lots of signposts along the way. And here's one vivid example, from crime novelist Robert Parker's fictional private detective Spenser, a Hall of Fame Old School guy who lived by a pithy code of honor:

Do what you say you will do.

Tell somebody you'll call them. Call. Tell folks you'll show up. Be there. Even if you don't feel like it. Old School people realize it's not all about them. They also know that, in real life, everybody doesn't get a trophy. Or deserve one.

To put it another way: say what you mean, and don't be a politically correct Snowflake. Don't call it "homegrown extremism" when it's Islamic jihad. And while we all want to breathe clean air and protect the environment—going back to Teddy Roosevelt, the Old School president who created the National Park System—don't

---

* Rod Serling was the creator of *The Twilight Zone*, an Emmy Award–winning science-fiction TV show that ran from 1959 to 1964. The opening narration, voiced by Serling, could easily be adapted for the present day: "You're traveling through another dimension. A dimension not only of sight and sound, but of mind. A journey into a bizarre land whose boundaries are that of indignation. Your next stop: the Snowflake Zone."

hector us about climate change while you fly around in private jets and have multiple houses with a carbon footprint the size of Kazakhstan.

So, if you're getting the impression that this book is going to lay down some rules about how to be Old School instead of a politically correct Snowflake, uh, that would be correct. Al Gore is not going to like it. Rosie O'Donnell will be disgusted. And don't even think about showing it to anyone at MSNBC.

On the other hand, Jack Nicholson might get a kick out of this book. He knows we need Old School people on that wall!

A final note about the curriculum: We hope this book will entertain you, and even define some aspects of life for you. And don't laugh that off. In order to really succeed in life, you have to have a personal philosophy. We hope this book points you in the right direction.

Old School Is in Session

There's probably no better display of Old School attitude than John Wayne's performance in the classic 1976 film *The Shootist*. It was Wayne's last film, and costarred Lauren Bacall, James Stewart, and Ron Howard.

The movie begins on January 22, 1901, when the legendary Wild West gunslinger J. B. Books, arrives in Carson City, Nevada, on the verge of dying from cancer. Books finds himself in a precarious situation: will he die from the disease, or will he be murdered?

Incredibly, in real life, John Wayne was actually dying from cancer as he filmed *The Shootist*. In fact, the disease would kill him three years later.

Back to the movie. Over the course of the next eight days, J. B. Books has to come to terms with his past, the present, and the choices he's made during his lifetime. He has to figure out how to

die with dignity, and also how to pass along some of the lessons he's learned: about right and wrong, and how to make your own way in the world with a code of honor, and ethics.

The town doctor (played by Stewart) can do nothing but medicate Books with laudanum. The Carson City marshal (played by Harry Morgan), wants the gunslinger out of town, and relents only when he finds out that Books is dying. He sends J.B. to a boarding-house run by a widow (Lauren Bacall), where he meets, and influences, her twenty-year-old son, Gillom, played by Ron Howard. In one scene, J.B. speaks to Gillom, imparting his core philosophy:

"I won't be wronged. I won't be insulted. I won't be laid a hand on. I don't do these things to other people, and I require the same from them."

In many ways, *The Shootist* is a perfect reflection of the way Wayne lived his life and the things he stood for. In fact, during the making of the film, the actor refused to do a scene that had been rewritten to have him shoot someone in the back. As he put it to the director, Don Siegel, "Mister, I've made over two hundred fifty pictures and have never shot a guy in the back. Change it."

John Wayne was not perfect. And viewed through the lens of 2017, he was very much a man of his time, with his views on Manifest Destiny (America's right to conquer the West) and stopping communism in Vietnam. But he loved America, and stood up for what he believed in—democracy over totalitarianism, the individual over the state, and robust self-reliance: nobody owes you anything. John Wayne knew that you make your own opportunities and create your own success—and he acted accordingly.

* * *

Another Old School guy is Billy Joel—but in a totally different way from John Wayne. Socially liberal, the diminutive Joel has sold more than 150 million records, earning himself a place in the Songwriters Hall of Fame.

What makes Billy Joel Old School?

Hard knocks, that's what.

Joel was raised in the working-class Hicksville section of Levittown, Long Island, not far from the Westbury section, where Bill O'Reilly grew up. They've known each other since they were young teenagers, when neither seemed likely to amount to anything in life, other than being known as a troublemaker.

Joel's father left his family when Billy was ten. His single mother raised him and his sister, and forced the rebellious Billy to take piano lessons at an early age. By the time he was in high school, where he was known as something of a hoodlum, he was already playing

piano in clubs on Long Island. He failed his final exams to graduate because he'd been out late playing a gig the night before.

Given his immense talent and the songs we've come to know and love, it might seem that Billy Joel was a natural to succeed, sooner or later, one way or another. But nothing could be further from the truth. He couldn't get a record deal; none of the big labels was interested in his music. He went to work as a fisherman to support himself, and even took up boxing—at first, to defend himself against the neighborhood tough guys, and later, to earn money, winning twenty-two fights on the Golden Gloves circuit, before quitting when his nose was broken during his twenty-fourth fight.

You may know the rest of the story—from his early success, to the management problems that left him nearly penniless, to the marriages, the divorces, the bouts with drugs and alcohol, and the ever-present battles against the snooty critics who dismissed his talent as middle-brow. Yet, in the face of all this—all the troubles, all the impediments, all the naysayers—he succeeded. He pulled himself together, cleaned himself up, and became a loving father, an international icon, a man who supports charities, veterans, and who has never forgotten where he came from, or his old friends—including O'Reilly, even to the point of making fun of his own foibles and ego with songs like "Big Shot" ("You had to be a big shot, didn't you? So much fun to be around").

It doesn't get much more Old School than that. Billy Joel believed in himself. He worked tirelessly to succeed. He never blamed his problems on anybody but himself. And no matter where he was performing, no matter how small or big the venue, he always worked hard to please his audience. And that's the real mark of Old School: Joel never pretended to be anything he wasn't, and never, ever, gave up—even when, truly, it would have been the easy thing to do.

* * *

This brings us to yet another singer who overcame almost impossible odds: the unstoppable, indomitable Tina Turner, a woman whose life story is as miraculous as her talent.

Tina Turner was born Anna Mae Bullock on November 26, 1939, on a farm in Nutbush, Tennessee, where her father oversaw sharecroppers who paid rent with the crops they grew. When World War II broke out, her father and mother moved to Knoxville to work in a defense factory, leaving Anna Mae and her sister behind, with their grandparents. The girls had only enough money to visit their parents twice during the war—which was also the first time that

Anna Mae sang for money, earning quarters at a woman's dress shop.

When the war was over, Anna Mae's parents split. Her father remarried and moved north; her mother briefly abandoned the family, leaving the girls with their grandmother. As a preteen, Anna Mae earned money working as a housekeeper. When her grandmother died, she was reunited with her mother in St. Louis, where she became a cheerleader in high school and planned to become a nurse at a local hospital, simply as a way to support herself. As she'd later tell it, it was during this period in St. Louis that she began to feel the pull of her talent and had the dream to perform. But there were lots of girls with good voices, and the odds of succeeding at or even earning a living doing what she loved seemed small in 1956.

Then, one night at a blues club in East St. Louis, she met Ike Turner. Her older sister had been dating a drummer in Ike's band, the Kings of Rhythm. Anna had waited for weeks, hoping for a chance to get onstage, to show what she could do. When she finally got the chance, singing a B. B. King song, Ike was so impressed that he immediately invited her to join the band.

Over the next twenty years, Ike and the now-renamed Tina got married and toured America and Europe, crossing over from black audiences to widespread, mainstream acclaim. It wasn't easy. They faced racism and prejudice, but they pumped out hit after hit, eventually opening for the Rolling Stones, who give Tina credit for teaching Mick Jagger how to dance.

Still, behind all the glamor and the glory, there were problems. Repeating the unfortunate experience of Tina's father's treatment of her mother, Ike was abusive. There were drugs and alcohol problems. Ike Turner was incredibly self-destructive and seemed determined to bring Tina down with him, even as she began to

enjoy success recording as a solo artist and as an actress in films like *Tommy*, where she plays the Acid Queen.

Finally, in 1976, after years of physical and emotional abuse, Tina Turner decided she'd had enough. She couldn't, and wouldn't, take it anymore. She ran out on Ike after a concert in Texas, with only a gas station credit card and thirty-six cents to her name. But she was determined to put her life back together, even it meant living on food stamps and cleaning friends' houses to earn money.

What happened next is the stuff of Old School legend—and is chronicled in the Oscar-nominated film *What's Love Got to Do with It*. Slowly, she rebuilt her career and her life. She toured with Lionel Ritchie and Rod Stewart, and then with the Rolling Stones again. Although her first post-Ike album failed, she went on to sell millions of records, and to costar with Mel Gibson in *Mad Max: Beyond Thunderdome.* She became one of the bestselling and most beloved artists of all time.

Needless to say, Tina Turner is Old School. Like Billy Joel, she worked for it. She didn't succeed because of a million Facebook friends or a sex tape. It was her talent, and her will and determination, that made it all happen—Old School values, Old School hard work. And to this day, no one has ever put on a better, stronger, or more exciting show.

But there's one more thing about Ms. Turner: she walked away from fame and money when she'd had enough. That's Old School thinking. She made a decision that ran counter to what many other people thought she should do. Tina Turner thinks for herself.

* * *

Finally, there's Chris Kyle, the legendary Navy SEAL who is credited with more enemy kills than any sniper in U.S. military history—and who was murdered by a fellow Iraqi war veteran who he was trying to help overcome the effects of posttraumatic stress disorder. You may have either read Kyle's book, *American Sniper: The Autobiography of the Most Lethal Sniper in U.S. Military History,* or seen the Oscar-winning movie based on his life, directed by Old School guy Clint Eastwood.

Chris Kyle was born in Midland, Texas, in 1974. His father, a deacon in the local church, gave Chris his first gun when he was eight. He grew up raising cattle and hunting deer, pheasant, and quail. After studying agriculture for two years at a local college, he dropped out to become a ranch hand and a professional bronco rider, until he shattered his arm at a rodeo show.

A longtime admirer of the military, Chris joined the Navy SEALs in 1999, and managed to get through the grueling training

despite the pins in his arm. From the very beginning, the SEALs were amazed by his skill as a marksman.

In the aftermath of 9/11 and the U.S. decision to topple Saddam Hussein, Chief Petty Officer Kyle served four tours of duty in Iraq. He killed more than 150 Iraqi insurgents. Wounded twice, he survived six separate IED attacks. He was so feared by the enemy that during his deployment to Ramadi, the insurgents began to call him Shaitan Ar-Ramadi, or the "Devil of Ramadi," and put a $21,000 bounty on his head that was eventually upped to $80,000. They even put up Wanted: Dead or Alive posters featuring his tattoos, in order to make it easier for insurgents to identify him.

Here's where Old School comes in.

The job of a sniper is to protect his fellow troops and to eliminate the enemy, as far away as possible, before he gets the chance to kill you or your men. There was nobody who did this better than Chris Kyle. He was idolized by his fellow soldiers for the way he protected them.

Just as notable is what Chris did *after* he was honorably discharged in 2009: he joined with FITCO Cares Foundation, a nonprofit that created the Heroes Project to provide fitness equipment, personal training, and psychological support to disabled veterans, families who'd lost a soldier, and vets suffering from posttraumatic stress disorder. Even as a civilian, Chris still loved his men, and was murdered because of that. In 2013 a deranged vet shot him dead in Texas. Chris left behind a widow and two children, ages eight and six.

In the end, what really made Chris Kyle Old school wasn't his gift as a marksman, his patriotism, his love of country, or even the medals he received for his service, including two Silver Stars, and five Bronze Stars. What really made Chris Kyle Old School was the way he looked at life and the way he looked after his guys.

Kyle understood there are people out there who threaten our way of life and want to kill us. And unlike former attorney general Loretta Lynch, he understood that terrorism and evil aren't going to be defeated with "compassion, unity, and love."

Perhaps the best way to sum up Chris Kyle's Old School values is to use his own words, from his book, *American Sniper*, explaining what he did and why: "I don't have to psyche myself up, or do something special mentally—I look through the scope, get my target in the cross hairs, and kill my enemy before he kills one of my people."

Snowdrift

So, there's O'Reilly, coaching Little League baseball on a cool May night. His team is one run down, and it's the last inning. Standing six foot four, O'Reilly is an imposing figure in the third base coach's box as he watches the base runner on second.

Suddenly, the batter hits a sharp ground ball past third base and into left field. O'Reilly bellows, "Go, go, go!" as his player heads for home plate. It's a lock; the game will soon be tied. But then, the unthinkable: the kid heading for home, a guy named Ian, stops running! Just stops. The ball is thrown to the catcher, and Ian is tagged out! Game over.

O'Reilly is stunned. Why would the kid have stopped running? O'Reilly's first instinct is to hustle over and ask the urchin for an explanation. But there are parents in the stands, some of whom have law degrees. O'Reilly is a famous guy who's every move is fodder for Internet sewer sites. So he subcontracts the confrontation out to another coach, who is five foot five.

"He says his leg hurt," the other coach reports to O'Reilly.

"He was six feet away from scoring. Did he pull a muscle?"

Both coaches then turn and look at Ian, who now is briskly walking away, his mother's arm around him, heading for the ice-cream truck.

Isn't even limping.

Later that night, O'Reilly approaches his son, one of Ian's teammates.

"What happened to Ian? Why did he stop running? It cost us the game!"

Slowly, the boy turns away from the most precious material thing in his life, a computer that's sitting on a small table. He looks his father squarely in the eye, and says, "Dad, it's not right to assess blame."

Confused and somewhat dazed by this bit of sagacity, O'Reilly replies, "We could have won that game."

To which the young boy says, "Do we have any ice cream?"

* * *

It was 1960, and Chubby Checker was twisting over to every bank in Philadelphia. But in Levittown, New York, Joe Spink's Little League team had no time for that kind of frivolity. They were headed for the playoffs, and Spink was obsessed. His jaw full of tobacco, the rumpled manager had his young players doing sliding drills and wind sprints.

The temperature was ninety-seven. A U.S. Marine recruiter took names for future reference.

Mr. Spink, as we called him, did not speak very much. Instead, he would yell and spit dark juice at you if you struck out.

On one scorching-hot afternoon, our catcher dropped to his knees drenched with sweat.

"What's the matter with youse?" Spink yelled from the bench.

"I think I'm gonna throw up," the catcher moaned.

"Don't do it with the mask on!" Spink hollered. "O'Reilly, can you catch? Get in there!"

All of us on the team loved baseball even if we didn't love Mr. Spink. No matter how hot, dusty, or humid it was, we'd be on the field. Kid got hurt, we'd carry him to the bench. No tragedy. Few parents attended the games because the basic point of Little League was *to get their boys the hell away from them*!

The twenty-five-dollar registration fee was more than worth it.

The Little League experience back in the days of Elvis as compared to the era of Justin Bieber is an excellent example of Old School versus Snowflake. Ian and many of his teammates will not likely have Navy SEAL training in their futures.

But O'Reilly's Old School upbringing steeled him to overcome many obstacles and gave him, shall we say, a unique view of life.

* * *

Living in Los Angeles with his wife and teenage twins, Feirstein has had his own baffling experiences with Snowflake culture.

One afternoon, picking up one of the twins from a school that prides itself on "inclusion, diversity, and respect," he noticed that the teen seemed unusually distant and unhappy—well beyond the normal resentment of having to go to school at all.

"What's bothering you?" Feirstein inquired. And, true to form, like any American kid answering a question posed by a parent, the teen gave Bruce exactly the reply he expected: "Nothing."

While the two were walking the dog later that night, however, the truth came out.

"So, what's bothering you?" Bruce asked a second time. "What's wrong?"

"Well," the teenager began reluctantly, "in my geography class, we were looking at a map of Los Angeles and looking for income inequality and standards of living in Los Angeles. And a classmate pointed at the map and said, "This is where the good people live . . . and this is where the bad people live: the rich people. They're greedy and selfish and have too much money and too many things and don't give any money to charity and don't care about anybody but themselves."

Feirstein already suspected where this was going. "And . . . ?"

"Our neighborhood is where the bad people live."

Feirstein cringed. How is this helpful? What is a kid supposed to learn from this? The Feirstein family isn't "rich" by Hollywood standards, but it isn't poor, either. Bruce and his wife both come from middle-class backgrounds, and have tried to pass those values on to their kids. They're never going to be mistaken for Kardashians.

"What did the teacher say?" Feirstein asked.

"She said it probably wasn't a good idea to categorize people that way."

Feirstein was glad that the teacher had corrected the other kid. That was a good thing. But it didn't fix the problem that his kid was still upset by what happened. The important thing, at that moment, was to figure out how to discuss it.

"Listen," Feirstein began, in a calm, reassuring voice, "whoever said that doesn't know anything about us. They don't know who we are, what we believe, how we made our money, or what causes and charities we support." He paused, then continued: "You can't generalize about anybody like that—whether it's the neighborhood they live in, the religion they practice, or the color of their skin. You've got to treat everybody with respect. And that's what I expect from you. Because the other way is just wrong."

"I know that, Dad," the kid replied, as if he didn't need to hear this.

"Good!" Feirstein exclaimed, feeling relieved, and added playfully, "Because that was an incredibly stupid thing for that kid to say."

To which the teenager replied, "Oh God, Dad! Do you have to be so *judgmental*?"

* * *

And so, we find ourselves in 2017, the era of the Snowflake, an age when everything has to be politically correct, a time when everybody expects a trophy and everyone gets to be outraged about everything, all the time.

Do you ever feel like you're living in an old episode of *Dragnet*, where Jack Webb's Sgt. Joe Friday is constantly warning, "Anything you say can, and will, be used against you"? Only, today, you can be sure it wouldn't be Sgt. *Joe* Friday—maybe Josephine, or José. Either way, the character would almost certainly not be played by Jack Webb, an Old School guy if there ever was one.

Just consider what's been happening on some of our college campuses.

• In October 2015, a lecturer at Yale University sent an e-mail to students saying she didn't think the school should be issuing rules and regulations about appropriate Halloween costumes. She didn't provide a detailed list of what was considered inappropriate, but it doesn't take a degree in advanced cultural studies to know what she was talking about: ethnic garb such as Native American headdresses, Mexican ponchos and sombreros, or Arabian robes and headscarves. The crime here is called "cultural appropriation," meaning that unless you're a member of a particular ethnicity, it's considered offensive and demeaning to borrow from that culture, even if you're doing so in a good-natured way.

The point of the Yale lecturer's e-mail was to suggest that college-age students should be responsible for making their own Halloween costume choices, for good or for bad.

Sounds reasonable, yes? Telling kids who are old enough to fight in wars that maybe they're mature enough to make their own choices about Halloween costumes? Yes, that's right: Halloween costumes!

And doesn't dressing up fall under freedom of expression?

Well, actually, no.

A group of Yale students reacted to the e-mail with a full-fledged meltdown, a veritable temper tantrum, demanding the resignation of the lecturer and her Yale professor husband and screaming that the two weren't protecting the students or making them feel safe at the $46,000-a-year (plus $14,000 for room and board) Ivy League school.

The upshot of all this? The students won. The lecturer resigned, and her husband gave up his position overseeing one of the colleges at Yale. All because of Halloween costumes.

• At Emory University in Atlanta (and a dozen other colleges and universities across the country), the mere sighting of "Trump 2016" in chalk on a sidewalk sent some students into a tizzy. Their angst stemmed from what are now called *microaggressions* and *hate speech*. Snowflakes alleged that any support of Trump was racist and divisive, triggering feelings of anxiety and fear. A student at Emory said, "I legitimately feared for my life."

• At University of Tennessee at Chattanooga, a newly elected member of the student senate was forced to resign after chalking Trump's name on a campus sidewalk. (Her fellow senate members said they couldn't stand by someone who supported bigotry and oppression.)

• At Appalachian State University, the provost said that Trump chalkings there had created "fear, hurt, anxiety and marginalization ... with language that was divisive, non-inclusive, and in direct opposition to civil discourse."

• At Emory, after meeting with protestors, the president acknowledged "the genuine concern and pain in the face of this perceived intimidation," and said he would be reviewing security camera recordings to see if any laws had been broken and promised that the school would take a number of significant steps to respond to students' concerns, including refining school policy and "creating opportunities for dialogue."

• At Oberlin College in Ohio (where tuition is $51,000, plus $14,000 for room and board), students expanded their protests beyond the usual charges of institutional racism, sexism, and lack of diversity to target the cafeteria, whose sushi, they declared, was racist (and guilty of cultural appropriation) because it hadn't been made with the right rice.

• At Brown University, in response to protests over a debate about rape culture, the school set up a "safe space" filled with cookies, coloring books, bubbles, Play-Doh, calming music, pillows, blankets, and a video of frolicking puppies for anyone who might find the comments at the debate "triggering" or the debate itself too upsetting to attend.

• In July 2016, Cleveland's Case Western Reserve University set up a safe space for students triggered by the Republican National Convention. And two weeks later, at the Democratic National Convention in Philadelphia, a young Bernie Sanders supporter told *Time* magazine that he and his friends were so upset by *macroaggressions* inside the hall that it prevented them from disrupting Hillary Clinton's historic acceptance speech.

• At the University of Missouri, the school's diversity office issued a primer on microaggressions, detailing the words and phrases that might be triggering or offensive, including the words *urban* and *Christmas vacation* and the phrases "America is a meritocracy," "Where did you go to high school?" "You speak English really well," and "Would you like to play golf?"

The list goes on and on—and begs the simple question: How are any of these Snowflake students ever going to function in real life?

5

Growing Up Old School

With a grandfather who saw combat in World War I and later walked a beat in Brooklyn for the NYPD, O'Reilly is an expert in Old School home procedure. Add to that a father who was a naval officer in World War II, and you have an upbringing that would send Susan Sarandon screaming into the night.

Let's start with food. Because my father and mother lived through the horror of the Great Depression, the ultimate Old School shaper, dining at home was an intense experience. "Cleaning your plate" was the order du jour.

Easier said than done.

That's because most of the food my mother served was gruesome.

SpaghettiOs on Monday. Brutal. Little round pasta pieces with a red sauce that could remove paint.

Tuesday was boiled hot dogs. We did have a primitive grill, but my mom loved that scalding water. Even Barney, my German shepherd, who would eat a rat, passed on the boiled meat.

Wednesday was usually pot roast. You had to cut it with a chain saw.

By Thursday, starvation would begin to set in, so my sister and I would wolf down the entree, Hamburger Helper, because we knew what was coming on Friday.

Fish sticks.

"What kind of fish is this," I once asked my father.

Immediately, an Old School reply came back: "Barracuda. What do you care?"

Help was not forthcoming.

Like many Americans back in the 1950s and '60s, my family did not have much money. This was reflected in the used Nash Rambler parked in our driveway, and the failure of my parents even to consider buying an air conditioner, which made the summer months that much more enjoyable.

Also, we had just one bathroom—if you don't count the bushes in our tiny backyard.

My upbringing was Old School for one major reason: my sister and I basically accepted the situation and fell into line. We did not "fight the power," as the Isley Brothers once suggested.

Not that we had much choice.

I will, however, confess to feeling supreme envy when watching the TV sitcoms on our black-and-white TV. *Leave It to Beaver* was big. Dopey kid, kind of dense older brother named Wally, mother who dressed like Queen Elizabeth, and a dad who often wore a tie to dinner.

Fantasy island before *Fantasy Island*.

One time, I decided to give my father some jazz. "Dad, you should be wearing a tie for supper."

"Why?"

"Because Mr. Cleaver does."

Confusion creased my dad's face.

"Who?"

"Beaver's father."

"That kid on TV? Is that what you're talking about?"

"Yeah."

My father paused and put down the book he was reading (Old School leisure activity).

"So, let me break this to you, son. Any father who allows his kid to be called 'Beaver' should be put in an insane asylum."

Hard to argue with Old School logic.

* * *

Feirstein's experience with the Old School mode of "adolescent behavior adjustment" appears to be different from O'Reilly's, but in many ways it's exactly the same.

I grew up in Maplewood, New Jersey, a beautiful tree-lined town twenty miles west of Manhattan that could have passed for the suburban version of *The Andy Griffith Show*. Packs of kids rode bicycles in the streets. There were fireworks and a parade on July 4. The librarians knew your name. The police were your friends and your neighbors.

Back in the 1960s, Maplewood had a reputation as an affluent town. Like most supposedly affluent towns, even Beverly Hills, Maplewood had a good side and a not-so-good side.

The swells lived "up the hill"—lawyers, stock brokers, and a reputed Mafia chieftain.

And then there was the other side of the town, at the bottom of the hill, on the wrong side of the railroad tracks—where the Feir-stein family lived in a three-bedroom house with one bathroom (just like O'Reilly) and neighbors who worked as engineers at Bell Telephone, landscape foremen on the Garden State Parkway, and, in at least one or two cases, "goodfellas" who worked as part of the crew for the wiseguy up the hill.

I have never forgotten my first day at South Orange Junior High School, when one of the so-called greasers shook me down for lunch money in the school cafeteria. The kid snapped his fingers, held out an open palm, smiling like a shark, and said, "Yo, Feirstein. Show me a *dime!*"

It was an Old School shakedown.

I promptly handed over the cash.

My father was a Purple Heart World War II veteran who'd served in the army, fighting in France and Germany. After that, he sold textiles in Manhattan. My mother was a first-grade teacher at an elementary school in Newark, directly across from an apartment where Cory Booker would live years later when he became mayor of that city.

My father and mother were both children of immigrants who fled to America to escape religious persecution in Romania and Austria, respectively. They were the first in their families to gradu-ate from college. And like O'Reilly's parents, they both grew up dur-ing the Depression and were forever careful with money.

But there was something else that hung over the family.

Like all Jewish families back then, even ones that weren't par-ticularly religious, they were deeply affected by the Holocaust.

My younger sister, Andrea, and I were born within a decade or so of the discovery of the Nazi death camps.

It didn't come up every day, but it was always there, the same way, almost sixteen years later, 9/11 still hangs over New York City.

To this end, Feirstein's parents taught their children Old School values by setting examples: They voted in every election. They filled the house with books and magazines and newspapers. They served on school district committees and volunteered at the local library.

They didn't need to spell it out, but they taught their children how lucky they were to live in America, and how important it was to be part of the community and to participate in our democracy.

This isn't to say that life in the Feirstein household was all civics lessons and politics. Far from it.

We worked. Our basement was filled with so many hammers, saws, power tools, and toxic chemicals that the EPA and OSHA would have turned a profit, handing out fines.

If a room in that house needed painting, we painted it.

If a ceiling fixture needed to be replaced, my father climbed on a ladder and taught me how to rewire it.

Being helpless in the Feirstein house was unthinkable. If you owned a bicycle, you were expected to know how to maintain it. If you shattered a windowpane, you were expected to know how to replace it. You didn't dare call a plumber to replace a fifteen-cent faucet washer.

If there was a side benefit to all this—even beyond learning the Old School value of self-reliance and giving me the skills eventually to join a construction crew rehabing tenements in Boston to help pay for college—it was that it taught me to curse like an Old School sailor, with style, effect, and Olympic gold medal distinction.

Summer was Boy Scout camp, learning about "the great outdoors" before it was renamed "the environment."

Two weeks in an army surplus tent, throwing hatchets, starting campfires, building teepees, studying "Indian lore," canoeing without a life vest, and target shooting with .22 caliber rifles.

And all that was *between* the twice-daily American flag

ceremonies (up at dawn, down at dusk, accompanied by cannon fire!), marching in parade formation to John Philip Sousa military marches, praying before meals, eating endless USDA-surplus peanut butter sandwiches, and using outdoor latrines.

If somebody were crazy enough to try to run a camp like that today, you can be sure that somehow, somewhere some self-righteous father would figure out a way to stuff three ACLU lawyers and a personal injury attorney into his kids' duffel bag.

It's probably not altogether surprising that the Feirsteins and the O'Reillys ate from the same five basic food groups: fish sticks, hotdogs, frozen peas (did they come any other way?), beef of undetermined origin, and spaghetti—which nobody ever called "pasta" back then, unless you owned a restaurant.

Back in the pre-Snowflake era (which should probably more accurately be called the "pre-hipster, pre-artisanal mayonnaise years"), people would have thought you insane, or maybe speaking in tongues, if you used words like *vegan, gluten-free, low-carb, paleo-, low-sodium,* or *organic.*

The only known "diet" was the stuff they put down in front of you—and your only nutritional choices were to eat it or starve.

"Eating healthy" meant finishing everything on your plate.

If you'd asked for "free range chicken" or "free range beef," they would have looked at you as if you were speaking another language. "... Free? ... Range? You mean you want it barbecued???"

And "locally sourced" could mean only one thing: those pathetic tomatoes our family tried to grow in the back yard every single year.

Because my mother often worked late at school, she'd cook meals weeks in advance and toss them in the freezer, wrapped in aluminum foil and with a piece of masking tape on which she'd write down what was inside with a black Magic Marker.

One night, when I was a snarky fifteen- or sixteen-year-old, I said, "You know, Ma, one day, we're all going to get wiped out by some form of nuclear annihilation. And a hundred thousand years from now, when a new civilization evolves, they're going to find that the only thing that survived was your freezer. And they're going to open it and pull out one of your aluminum foil packages, utterly baffled, wondering if they've found the key to life, and ask, 'What is this . . .'meatballs for six"?' "

Across the table, my mother fixed me with a very Old School evil eye.

"I hope that someday you find a way to earn a living from that mouth of yours," she said. "Because I'm not feeding it anymore."

The Old School Guide to Modern Parenting

Are you in danger of bringing up a Snowflake? Or are you trying to bring up a child who can actually cope with the world? The following comparison chart may offer some helpful guidelines.

	OLD SCHOOL	SNOWFLAKE
What's the basic parent/child relationship?	Parent and child	Friends
How do you communicate?	Face-to-face	Text
Fourth birthday present?	Toys and stuffed animals	An iPhone
Child's greatest fear?	Getting a "time-out"	Low batteries
What should your child learn by the end of first grade?	Reading and writing	Critical thinking
And how does that manifest itself?	"See Spot run."	"Dick and Jane are animal rights activists who reject the corporatization of American pet culture."
Nightly ritual?	"Go do your homework."	"I'll be up in a minute to help you with your homework."
Is your child gifted?	Yes, at birthdays and Christmas.	Do you really have to ask?
Whose fault is it if your child is getting Cs and Ds in school?	The kid, for not working hard enough.	The teacher's, for not being sensitive to how special and gifted your child is and for not taking the time to be more nurturing.

(Continued)

Social

The year was 1962, and O'Reilly faced a brand-new challenge: talking to girls!

Catholic school girls, to be exact. There were thirty-five of them in my eighth-grade class at St. Brigid in Westbury, New York.

Most of these girls had been my classmates since first grade, but now young lady status had arrived. Of course, the girls were far more mature than the boys in the class, many of whom rivaled Hun children in the social grace department.

Our teacher, Sister Mary Martin, was very Old School when it came to socializing. When the big eighth-grade dance was announced, the nun brought forth this pearl while discussing slow dances: "Leave room for the Holy Spirit!"

Confusion broke out. Was the third part of the Trinity actually

	OLD SCHOOL	SNOWFLAKE
And what do you blame for that?	Video games	An antiquated, results-oriented school system that doesn't foster creativity
So how do you deal with that?	Take away the video games and tell the kid to work harder.	Confront the school administration and bring in some lawyers.
If your kid is away at college, how often do you communicate?	Weekly, by phone	Hourly, by text
What's the first thing that comes to mind when you hear the term *helicopter parent*?	Uncle Bob, who flew missions in Afghanistan	"What do you mean, I'm too involved with my kid's life? I just want to make sure everything is perfect!"
In one sentence, describe your worldview?	"There is both good and evil in this world."	"There's no such thing as right or wrong."
Which means?	Life is not always fair.	Everybody *deserves* a trophy, and my kid should never be criticized for or suffer consequences from his bad behavior.
Finally, what's the one life-threatening experience you hope your kids will never have to face?	Jungle warfare in a military unit	Jungle gyms in a school yard

attending the dance? Why would he locate himself between two sweaty thirteen-year-olds to begin with?

The class hooligan, Clement, immediately raised his hand. "Sista, if we crush the Holy Spirit on the dance floor, is that a mortal or venial sin?"

Clement was swiftly removed from the room.

My parents rarely discussed the opposite sex with me, and the nuns would deflect any specific questions while pointing to the Inquisition. But Billy McDermott had all the answers because his older brother had a copy of *Playboy* magazine.

After listening to McDermott for ten minutes, I believed that in order to have sex, you'd have to smoke a pipe and wear pajamas in the daytime (a Hugh Hefner reference for you Snowflakes).

The truth is that while I backed down from no boy, girls frightened me. I couldn't shut up with my thug friends, but when Claire told me I had nice eyes, I barely got out a "thanks."

My first crush was Irene, in the fifth grade, and I showed my affection by hitting her with an apple. Didn't mean it; I was aiming for Salvatore Modica. Didn't matter. Irene was deeply offended, and another kid told Sister Carolyn, who whacked me on the wrist with a ruler.

Today, the good sister would be doing community service.

My mother offered a few hints before the dance. She told me that the boy should approach the girl and softly say, "Would you like to dance?"

Sounds simple. It wasn't.

What if Bernadette or Susan said something like "No, thanks, Billy, I'd rather socialize with a salamander."

So, most of the guys, including me, were paralyzed by fear. That gave the two or three junior Hefners in the class free rein to have fun at the dance while the rest of us stood around watching our classmates do the Twist.

Now for a serious Old School point. When it came to girls, some of the boys got a little too taken with themselves. A few years later, pregnancies started happening in the neighborhood. They were usually hushed up, but we all knew. One of my cousins married a seventeen-year-old local girl. Their first baby was born seven months later. That scenario was not uncommon back then. Abortion was not an option for most.

I avoided all dating drama because I really didn't begin going out with ladies until the summer before my eighteenth birthday. Until then, I was busy playing sports and working after school. Not much time for wooing (Old School word).

One humid July night, a pretty girl named Marie accepted my invitation to see the rerelease of *Gone with the Wind*, a film that seemed to run for seven hours. Lots of wide shots of Civil War people milling around before Clark Gable's character finally figured out that Vivien Leigh's was a loon.

As the movie ended, we had just enough time to go to Jann's ice-cream shop before Marie had to be home. Like my grandfather, her dad was an Irish cop. I walked her to the door ten minutes early.

That's right, I walked her to the door and, at seventeen, she still had a curfew. Old School. Also, I got a soft kiss. It was nice.

Just ahead, Feirstein and I will chronicle today's dating world. Hint: it's often grim, and driven by compulsive texting centered on "hooking up."

One final image of the Old School dating scene: if you've never seen the TV show *American Bandstand*, look it up. There's video around. That program defined teen America in the 1960s and featured Dick Clark, a man with hair that never moved.

American Bandstand, *1958. No twerking allowed!*

Bandstand was the trendsetter all across the USA. Today, many young Americans would mock it, sneering at the social conformity the show embraced.

But ask yourself this: are kids better off now?

Now, let's hear what Feirstein has to say about this.

* * *

Ah, William. My "social" awakenings—which in the movie business are called coming-of-age stories—are pretty much the same as yours, minus the nuns and the Catholic stuff: slow-dancing to

Gerry and the Pacemakers' "Don't Let the Sun Catch You Crying," the trading of sacred ID bracelets, the furtive, fumbling first kiss.

In my case, this last item involved beer at a friend's house while his parents were away on vacation. I was around fourteen years old. While I don't remember the girl's name, I'll never forget her reaction: "Ugh," she said with a scowl. "You taste like beer." Since then, I've always associated beer with that night, and never really grew a taste for it. I'm not sure if that's Old School, but those things do tend to leave their mark on you.

When I first started writing for magazines and the movie business, believe it or not, I wrote about dating. Sure, O'Reilly was off in the bush somewhere, wearing a safari jacket covering wars. But I was writing about what I knew. And what I was living through at the time.

In a nod to the Old School style of reporting, I pretty much lived in a singles bar in Manhattan for a month, trying to figure out, for *New York Magazine*, how a bar opens and becomes "the hottest place in town." Also, how the mating ritual worked among singles on First Avenue in New York City. (Short answer: The bartenders gave away free drinks to women, and everyone got more attractive as the night went on.)

Not long after that, I wrote a book titled *Nice Guys Sleep Alone: Dating in the Difficult Eighties*, whose premise was that (a) dating is difficult, and (b) even though we were supposedly living in an age of no-strings-attached sex, if you went to bed at night with a date, you woke up the next morning with a relationship.

Hollywood bought both the book and the singles bar article to be turned into movies. I wrote the scripts, which were romantic comedies, but the movies never got made.* Still, I learned some important lessons from the book, about dating and journalism.

When *Nice Guys* was published, it was selling well in New York, Los Angeles, Chicago, and San Francisco, but nowhere else. I couldn't figure out why it wasn't moving in the rest of the country. Then, one night, after a book signing in Cheyenne, Wyoming, a grizzled old lawyer explained it to me.

"Son," he said, "you've got a job, two arms, two legs, and I assume the rest of your vital parts are in good working order. Dating just ain't that hard."

Then he went on to inform me that "In the rest of America, if you pulled the stunts you were writing about in New York City, you'd be run out of town. Sooner or later, somebody at the church, or the senior partner in your law firm, or even the foreman on your plumbing crew would tell you it's time to settle down—and to stop screwing around with our daughters."

It was a vital Old School piece of wisdom, direct from an Old School lawyer in the heart of the Old West, where church groups and community values still held sway.

Equally important, the cowboy lawyer taught me something about thinking that my own experiences were universal. Sometimes they are; sometimes they aren't. But I'm now suspicious anytime I read that "everybody" is following some new trend—whether

---

* Like most working screenwriters in Hollywood, I've written a lot of scripts that didn't get made into movies. The reason can be anything from the script to the budget to a studio executive's nineteen-year-old daughter announcing at the breakfast table that adult dramas, historical epics, or teenage angst films are "*so over.*" In other words, it's a long-shot business. And the chances of getting a studio film made are only slightly better than the odds of a meteor crashing through your roof and killing you before you finish reading this sentence.

it's "Everybody is sleeping around," "Everybody is hooking up," or "Everybody is watching Lena Dunham's show, *Girls*." Because what you usually find out later is that "everybody" means everybody the writer had dinner with that week.

Dating today is an entirely different world, and I can't imagine trying to make sense of it as a journalist. Forget about fix-ups, flirting, and flowers. It's all gone high-tech, with dating services like Match.com, sexting, and "hook-up" apps (read: one-night stand facilitators) like Tinder, where you swipe right on a stranger's picture if you're attracted, or left to send someone into the digital abyss.

It's all a *very* long way from the nuns at Catholic high school dances, Gerry and the Pacemakers, and the fear a young man felt when he rang the front doorbell to meet a girl's father before he took her out on a date.

Still, as observers of all this, your humble correspondents *do* have some Old School advice to pass along to our soon-to-be dating teenage offspring.

1) *The Internet is forever. So are naked pictures.* You may *think* that trading nude photos and sending X-rated texts is nothing but innocent flirting. That would be naïve. We live in the Internet age, where nothing, not even top-secret CIA briefings, stay secret. Don't take our word for it. Instead, let's go with paraphrasing Shakespeare: Hell hath no fury, and surely no more vicious broadband connection, than a lover scorned. Somehow, somewhere, all that stuff is going to come out and get passed around. And odds are you're *not* going to end up like Kim Kardashian, whose sex tape brought her fame, fortune, and a marriage to Kanye West. (On the other hand, maybe the mere thought of ending up in the Kardashian

family, married to West, is enough to scare you from stripping for the camera in the first place. In which case, congratulations: You're already in possession of some sensible Old School values.)

2) *Beware of infinite choices.* Can you really find true love by swiping right on Tinder? Can you really find "the One" amid the millions of digital personalities on Match.com? Yes, it has happened. But beware, sifting through all the fake and less-than-truthful profiles can give you a false sense of hope and possibility. We're not suggesting you settle for the thrice-married parent of six who lives next door. But the idea that there's always somebody better out there—somebody who's your perfect match and soul mate, just one more swipe away—may set you on the fastest ten-year journey you'll make to living alone in a studio apartment with cats.

3) *There is no such thing a "friend with benefits."* This is something that never changes. Somebody always wants more; somebody always has different hopes and expectations for the future. Sure, you can point to exceptions, but as a general rule, it's only in romantic comedies that in just under one hundred minutes of film time, the friends with benefits discover that they're perfect for each other.

4) *Too much information.* There's a trend in newspapers, magazines, and blogs to publish first-person tell-alls detailing every aspect of one's sex life. These pieces are written mainly by young women, but occasionally young men chime in, too. One sentence of advice: *Don't do this.* Like everything else on the Internet, this kind of confessional will linger there forever, just

waiting to embarrass you. Old School rule: Do not talk about your personal life with strangers.

5) *No means no.* It would be easy to make fun of all the hoops college administrators expect their students to jump through today before they engage in any kind of intimacy. But there's no middle ground here. It's all about the Old School tenets of respect and responsibility. No means no.

6) *The waiter rule.* In Feirstein's 1986 book about dating, he wrote, "Always watch the way someone treats a waiter on your first date. Because that's the way they're going to be treating you in six months." The point is as true today as it was back then: Never let anyone treat you badly. That's Old School.

A Brief History of Old School

To quote Ronald Reagan, "The struggle goes on. To be alive and to be human is to struggle for what is right and against what is not."

June 7, 10,000 BC: Men discover fire. Two days later, they invent barbecue. Twelve thousand years after that, Snowflakes will cite this as the beginning of man-made climate change.

1632: Galileo Galilei confirms that Earth revolves around the sun. Despite there being a "99 percent scientific consensus" about this, modern-day Snowflakes deny it, believing that, in fact, the world revolves around them.

March 23, 1775: Demanding independence from British rule, Patrick Henry declares, "Give me liberty or give me death." Two hundred thirty years later, the Snowflake generation echoes this fervent cry against oppression with "Give me safe spaces and trigger warnings!"

AD 1190: First recorded use of the adage "Rome wasn't built in a day," opening the door for the first Old School contractor to quip, "That's because I wasn't on the job."

Prehistoric times	500 BC	500 AD	1500 AD	1600	1700

541 BC: The first two-story house is built in Greece. Kids read about god Zeus on stone tablets. First recorded instance of Old School father calling up the stairs, "Put those tablets away and go to bed! Don't make me come up there!"

October 12, 1492: Columbus lands in the New World. Sets the stage for a culture that eventually supports, feeds, houses, and maintains tens of thousands of Snowflake college professors, who will declare this to be one of the worst events in history.

July 4, 1777: Americans celebrate their first Independence Day with Chinese-invented fireworks and hotdogs invented in Germany. Somewhere in the future, this will all be dismissed by Snowflakes as an "exercise in cultural appropriation."

1829: Abraham Lincoln splits rails in Illinois. Snowflakes will miss the Old School lesson about hard work and instead see this as Lincoln's endorsement of the anti–fossil fuel movement and of the need for Americans to abandon their automobiles and fund more public transportation projects.

June 4, 1940: Winston Churchill delivers his "We Shall Fight on the Beaches" speech to the British House of Commons. Seventy-five years on, Snowflakes still don't understand that while the "Arc of moral universe is long but it bends toward justice," somebody actually needs to get out there and *bend it.*

October 28, 1886: The Statue of Liberty is dedicated. Seventeen years later Emma Lazarus's ringing words are engraved upon its pedestal: "Give me your tired, your poor, your huddled masses yearning to breathe free." Snowflake response: Not nearly inclusive enough. As of this writing, 16 federal agencies and 237 special interest groups are still working to find an acceptable rewrite.

February 20, 1962: "Godspeed, John Glenn." Really? God? NASA? Had Snowflakes existed back then, they would have gone into full meltdown mode for this mixing of religion and government.

| 1800 | 1900 | 1950 | 1975 | 1990 |

March 17, 1930–May 1, 1931: The Empire State Building goes up in just under fourteen months. An Old School triumph of skill, determination, and thousands of Old School workers who erect four floors daily . . . and never once ask for the "vegan lunch" choice.

1974–1975: In an early precursor to fake news, *Time*, *Newsweek*, and dozens of newspapers run alarming stories about the oncoming ice age. Old School parents see this as an opportunity to teach their children about "snow-shovel-ready" jobs.

August 1945: With the dropping of "Fat Man" and "Little Boy," World War II ends. Can there be any doubt that, somewhere, a Snowflake professor has written an academic paper decrying not only the use of these atomic weapons, but also their names . . . for sexism and body shaming?

August 1996: The e-mail era begins. Luddite Old Schoolers quickly learn about Russian brides, Nigerian banking transfers, and the dread Reply All button. On the bright side, they start buying all their childhood toys on eBay.

June 26, 2015: The Supreme Court legalizes gay marriage. Old Schoolers ask, "Why do politicians insist on saying they've 'evolved' on issues instead of just admitting, 'I've changed my mind'?"

December 2000: Old Schoolers vow never to hear the expressions "hanging chad," "butterfly ballot," or "selected, not elected" ever again.

November 12, 2016: In perhaps the most egregious example of PC culture run amok, faculty and students at the Thomas Jefferson–founded University of Virginia demand that the president of UVA stop quoting Jefferson in her e-mails. To her great Old School credit, the UVA president, Teresa Sullivan, quotes Jefferson when she overrules them.

March 9, 2010: Old Schoolers are baffled when Nancy Pelosi says, "We have to pass the bill so that you can find out what is in it." Old Schoolers would have read the bill first.

December 2016: Bernie Sanders admits that political correctness played a role in Hillary Clinton's loss of the presidential election.

2000	2010	2015	2020

October 2008: The financial meltdown. While the rest of the world struggles to understand "subprime mortgages" and "credit default swaps," Old Schoolers take pride in having, and understanding, something called a "savings account."

2013: Visiting a football field–size office in Silicon Valley, an Old Schooler realizes that the only difference between the sweatshops of 1910 and the tech industry of 2013 is that instead of slaving over sewing machines, these people were slaving over computers.

January 2025: Self-driving cars are due to go on sale in the United States. Correct Old Schooler reaction: "No. Friggin'. Way."

7

Going to
Old School

Graduating elementary school did not change O'Reilly's nitwit status. The year was 1963, President Kennedy had come through the Cuban Missile Crisis, and Camelot was in full swing. That summer, no one had any idea that Lee Harvey Oswald would strike in November.

Back in Levittown, my crew played stickball during the day and sang Beach Boy tunes in the evening. We also went to the town pool and, for the first time, noticed those yellow polka dot bikinis that Brian Hyland was singing about. The teenage years were beginning.

My father and mother were not involved with any of this. They insisted I be home for dinner around 6:30, but that was it. The kids were on their own as far as recreation was concerned. The old adage had changed to "Children should be neither seen nor heard."

One exception to the parental day-to-day indifference: if it rained, no sane parent wanted hooligan kids inside their home. So, they dropped us off at the movie theater, where double features occupied us urchins for almost four hours. My favorites included *The Blob* and *House on Haunted Hill.*

By the way, I had known Steve McQueen was going to be a major star when I saw him earnestly save his Pennsylvania town from the vicious, uncaring Blob. That was not an easy task.

Anyway, most of my friends were going to attend the local public high school in the fall, and that's where I wanted to go. But my father astutely figured out that I would be headed straight to "shop" class because I was not exactly reading Plato in my spare time. The public school quickly segregated the incoming students according to academic potential. It would have been welding for me.

So, my dad swung into action. The guidance counselor at a nearby Catholic high school, Chaminade, in Mineola, was a friend of the family, so I got into the school through the back door. Chaminade was, and remains today, a rigorous academic place. Plus, you had to wear a jacket and tie *every day.* I could not master a knot, so I wore a clip-on.

I hated Chaminade—loathed it, cursed it, and dreamed of burning it down. While my thug friends walked to the public school, often smoking Kool cigarettes on the way, I had a forty-minute bus ride through the streets of Long Island. While my pals wore sneakers and leather jackets like Brando, I wore wing tips. While they went to the soda shop after school to flirt with pretty girls, I got back on a stuffy bus totally devoid of girls. Why? Because Chaminade was an *all-boys* school, that's why!

After the first few weeks, I sarcastically said to my father, "Can't I just join the Marines instead?"

He actually brightened up. "When you're seventeen. I already have the paperwork."

Chaminade did not mess around. Even minor infractions got you kicked out. No greased-back hair, no gum chewing, and no Kools, anywhere. If they smelled tobacco on you—sayonara! That's Japanese for good-bye. Chaminade "men" didn't have to learn Japanese, but we did have to take Latin. Even though nobody on the planet speaks Latin, and the likelihood of ever using the language in any interaction with another human being is infinitesimal, we had to memorize the entire language. Why? Because learning Latin instills *discipline*!

And there it is: discipline, a key Old School value. Even though my father was tough, he knew I lacked vision and fortitude (another good Old School word). He understood that his son was not going to break out of the working class unless there was a big change.

Chaminade was a big change.

Let's start with three hours of homework. Are you freakin' kidding me? I thought. How am I going to keep up with David and Ricky Nelson? Or listen to Elvis? Or watch *The Untouchables*? They even gave us homework on the weekends, and if you didn't do it, they kept you after class until you did!

Chaminade was modeled after Alcatraz.

So, I did it. I had no choice. During the day, I had to deal with the Catholic brothers who controlled the school. At night, my father loomed. There was no escape. There was only pain.

I got through it and was accepted by a few colleges. Notre Dame turned me down, so I decided on Marist College, a small school in Poughkeepsie, New York, populated mostly by working-class students like me. Marist was my choice because I thought I might have a chance to make the football team as a freshman, which I did. But that never would have happened if not for that Chaminade discipline. Although I played ice hockey, not football, in high school, I could throw and kick the ball very far. A gift I wanted to use.

The preseason football camp at Marist began three weeks before classes commenced. In August, Poughkeepsie averages about 102 degrees, right behind Yuma, Arizona. The coach thought it wise to schedule two practices a day, so that the weaker players would die, thereby saving him the angst of cutting them from the team.

It is simply impossible to describe how much fun we all had on a dirt field with little water for almost four hours every hot, humid day. We had Iwo Jima–type fun, root canal joviality.

But, again, I got through it.

That's because I had acquired discipline. I could handle a good amount of pain, both physical and mental.

No question, Snowflakes would have melted in three minutes on that dusty field.

When classes began, I experienced another revelation. I knew almost all the stuff. I had learned it at Chaminade. While many of my fellow students couldn't write two consecutive sentences without using a double negative, I knocked out the assignments quickly and with aplomb. Only a B student in high school, I was cruising in college. Presto! The light went on: all the pain I'd endured at Chaminade might have been worth it.

Also, while many of my fellow freshmen smoked and drank themselves into a stupor, I did not. For the first time in my life, I was focused on achievement and felt absolutely no need to chug a brewsky. Somehow, throwing up in my dorm room was not wildly attractive. To this day, I do not drink.

But rejecting freshman madness wasn't easy, and to avoid being labeled a wuss, I had to socialize while at the same time avoiding felonious behavior. Thus, decisions had to be made.

In the spring of my freshman year, I was invited to join the

Moon Platoon, which, despite the name, was not an astronomy club. Against my better judgment, I attended the platoon's first meeting. It took place on the banks of the Hudson River, which flanked the campus. Kegs of beer were present at midday—never a good sign.

As platoon members filled their cups, a ship appeared in the distance. It was the *Hudson Dayliner,* traveling upriver from New York City until it reached the Franklin Roosevelt estate in Hyde Park, where it would then turn around and sail back.

As the riverboat approached the college, the Moon Platoon guys began lining up and waving. I stepped back, not really understanding the play that had been kept secret from the new recruits.

The happy tourists waved back. Then, all at once, a whistle sounded and about two dozen American college students turned their backs on the *Dayliner* and dropped their pants.

Horror is too slight a word to describe the reaction on the boat.

Now, it *was* funny, no question. Even though I didn't participate, I laughed along with the other morons. But some Old School value whispered into my puerile mind, "This is stupid and offensive, O'Reilly. Little kids can see that. What is wrong with you?"

Despite urging from the leader of the platoon, a student nick-named Squatty-body, I declined to sign up. Even at age nineteen, I knew that that kind of activity was not going to be a résumé enhancer. By the way, because of the Moon Platoon, the riverboat company eventually changed the vessel's route, turning the boat around at the Mid-Hudson Bridge so it would not have to pass the college again.

After finishing two years at Marist, I had another decision to make: should I apply for the third-year-abroad program? I did, and was promptly rejected. But my grades were far above the threshold needed. So why did I get passed over?

Word came back: my personality was too rough. Translation:

your Levittown upbringing was not genteel enough to risk sending you to the University of London.

Pondering the situation, I reacted from a deep intellectual place: "Blank you, Jack. I've got the grades, and my father knows a lawyer" (which would have been news to him had he been told, which he wasn't).

After a battery of interviews, I made it clear that I was not going to let the issue go. Truth is, I didn't really care that much about living in England, because I had a chance to start as quarterback my junior year. Still, the Old School tenet of not accepting insults drove me to torture the guy in charge of the abroad program. He finally relented, telling folks the campus would be better without me—most likely true—and that I could go overseas.

One problem: my father had to pay for the travel.

Here's that phone call:

"Dad, I'm thinking about going abroad."

"Good, join the ROTC."

"No, it means I'll do my junior year going to school in London."

"Why?"

"Ummm. Maybe I'll learn a lot."

"What about football?"

"I know, but this might be a good opportunity."

My father saw it and made it happen. I never told him about the Levittown slight. The truth is, I was a blunt, tough-talking guy with a *Saturday Night Fever* accent. I might have rejected the Moon Platoon, but sending me anywhere near cultured people might have damaged the college's rep. But Old School folks don't like to be told they can't do something they have earned the right to do.

Hello, Big Ben.

The two semesters in London changed me for the better. It took about a month for me to adjust to steak and kidney pie and fish and chips that took three days to digest. But once I had a good look around at my new circumstances, I started to understand the big picture: it's a complicated, fascinating world that should be explored.

Bottom line: Old School values of discipline, reasonable conduct, and not letting anybody insult you led me to a successful college experience.

This, in turn, allowed me to pursue a great career. Old School, baby. That was my ticket to a lifetime of adventure.

Over to you, Feirstein.

* * *

In the spring of 1974, I was hanged in effigy at Boston University.

In the rearview mirror of 2017, this would probably be seen as a pretty big deal by most people, and possibly the most significant thing that happened to me during my four years at BU.

But not to Bill O'Reilly.

Because I'm willing to bet that *he'd* tell you the most significant thing that happened to me at BU was meeting . . . Bill O'Reilly.

Even then, I'm pretty sure he saw his life as one "Impact Segment" after another. Or maybe he just saw me as an "Unresolved Problem." Or maybe both.

Before I explain how these momentous events came to pass— meeting O'Reilly and getting hanged in effigy—let me backtrack a little.

Entering my senior year in high school in 1971, I had no idea what I wanted to do with my life. I was playing bass in a rock band. I was the business manager of the high school newspaper, selling, writing, and designing ads with pithy headlines for local stores and restaurants. I was also fixated on politics, as was everyone else I knew, with Richard Nixon in the White House and the war still raging in Vietnam. But as far as a career went—what I might study in college and actually *do* for the rest of my life—I was clueless.

After subtle prodding from my father—I remember him invoking the words *failure, ditch digger,* and *McDonald's*—I made an appointment to see the high school guidance counselor, a stern woman, probably in her mid-thirties, who also coached soccer and taught Driver's Ed.

"So, what do you want to be when you grow up?" she asked, already having informed me that my chances of getting into a school like Harvard or Yale were zero.

"Umm . . . I don't know," I answered, with all the poise and confidence an eighteen-year-old can summon. "Maybe a . . . political scientist?"

She looked at me as if I were speaking Swahili. "Do you have any idea what a political scientist does?"

"Ummm . . . no," I replied.

"Well, so long as you're interested in *science*, I think you should major in engineering," she said. This was both hilarious and inappropriate, as I was getting Cs in algebra and could barely do long division. (Unbeknownst to either of us, I was dyslexic. To this day, I still can't dial a long-distance phone number without inverting some of the digits.)

At home later that night, my parents weighed in with their own Old School value that "the teacher is always right." (It's an Old School rule that I don't necessarily agree with anymore, especially when the line gets blurred between education and indoctrination.) So, I applied to schools like Lehigh University and BU, planning to major in engineering. And to everyone's shock, I got in.

Then everything changed.

On a snowy Wednesday night in February 1971, I was helping to publish our high school newspaper, the *Columbian*, at a printing plant in Maplewood. I'd written and designed the ads, and was working at a light table with razor blades and rubber cement to position the news stories and format the pages. The room was filled with the clickety-clack of linotype machines and IBM composers churning out text and the cool, carbon scent of damp ink on freshly printed newspaper.

As we locked down the final page, it hit me: this is what I wanted to do with my life. Maybe journalism. Or advertising. But definitely communications. And I needed to find program at one of the colleges I'd been accepted to, fast.

Racing home, I tore through the college catalogs and found that Boston University had a school of communications. Two days later, I was flying to Boston. It's was the first time I'd ever been on an airplane. The cost was twenty dollars, on the Eastern Airlines Shuttle. And within ten minutes of walking on Commonwealth Avenue, I knew I was home.

Seven months later, in September 1971, I entered BU as a freshman. And it was during those first few weeks, with the crisp chill of early autumn in the air that I learned an Old School lesson that has guided me through the rest of my life.

Walking around the third floor of the student union, I passed an open door marked "Daily Free Press." Inside was a beautiful senior who was clearly upset and frustrated. She was the business manager of BU's student-run daily newspaper, and she wanted to quit.

After five minutes of conversation, I took her job. A year later, I was the editor in chief.

So, here's the vital Old School lesson: If somebody opens a door for you, walk through it. Life is random. You never know where anything might lead. And it might just be God's way of offering you an opportunity you shouldn't pass up.

But let's get back to BU.

At the end of my sophomore year, it was time to turn the paper

O'Reilly scrambles as quarterback for the Daily Free Press *football team.*

over to the next editor. I needed to sleep, and I needed a paying job. But I was smitten with newspapers, and couldn't give it up altogether.

The following year, I started writing a weekly "humor" column. During my early years at the school, I had developed a reputation as a smart-ass. I knew I had a strange way of looking at the world. I was in the process of learning the difference between satire and cynicism, and how to be funny without being mean and saying the kind of blunt things that so ticked off my mother. In the newspaper column, I began to poke fun at BU's "Beautiful People," the students with hot cars, fancy apartments, shag haircuts, and platform shoes who were renting hotel rooms on weekends to throw parties.

They thought it was funny. But there was someone on campus who was not impressed.

Pecking out a column on an old manual typewriter in our offices one morning, I watched as a shadow fell across the keyboard.

I looked up . . . and up . . . and up to see a guy standing there with something between a scowl and smile on his face. He was clearly a few years older than me, and looked like a cross between an NFL running back and a Boston cop.

"Can I help you?" I asked timidly.

"Are *you* Feirstein?"

"Yeah. Why?"

He glanced down at what I was typing, and shook his head.

"You're not looking out for the folks," he declared.

Hesitating before I answered, I tried to process this. You're not looking out for the folks? Who calls anybody "the folks"?

Looking up again, I asked, "So who are these *folks*?"

"The graduate students and the commuters," he said. "Not the hippy-dippy types living it up in the dorms like *you*, Feirstein."*

The moment O'Reilly said it, I knew he was right. We never wrote about those students, and it was only later that I found out that he himself was a graduate student, going for a master's in broadcast journalism, returning to school after spending a few years out teaching high school.

"What's your name?" I asked.

"O'Reilly."

"Maybe you should write a column for us."

"Good idea," he said, as if it should have been evident from the moment he walked in the door.

---

* Just for the record, in all the years we've known each other, I don't think I've ever heard O'Reilly use my first name. I'm not even sure he knows it.

So off he went to meet with the new editor, a guy from Colorado named Bruce Smith, who promptly gave him a weekly column.

And how did he return this favor?

He went after me. His first column was about the "loony" undergraduate culture I was writing about. So, I decided to fire back. And thus began our weekly war of the words in print, during which we argued about politics, pot, and pop culture.

Neither of us has copies of those columns anymore. But I recall them beginning with compliments like "I hate to break Feirstein's bubble, *but . . .*" and "Far be it for me to criticize the esteemed O'Reilly, *but . . .*"

The key thing here is that I was a liberal, and O'Reilly's leanings were more conservative. But we were friends, and we never attacked each other personally.

It was a different time in America then, a time when journalists and politicians could actually befriend, and respect, someone on the other side of the political divide, instead of automatically demonizing them, vilifying them, and finding a way to pin a "Stalin" or "Hitler" label on them.

It's an Old School way of thinking that I can't help but feel we'd all do well to relearn: the idea that someone with a different upbringing, from a different part of the country, with a different outlook and a different viewpoint, might actually have something valid to say, something worth listening to.

All this more or less brings me back to where I started: getting hanged in effigy.

By the spring of 1974, the United States was no longer fighting in Vietnam, and the draft was over. But at BU, there was still a group of die-hard radicals who felt a twitch, like a muscle memory, to shut down the school every year just before finals. It was almost

A typical day at Boston University in the early 1970s—the newspaper where O'Reilly and Feirstein first met.

as if their calendars went from homecoming to spring break to "Let's riot!"

Late one afternoon, in a sort of a pregame warm-up to shutting down the school the next day, they marched on campus chanting, "All Boston University / Must go Communist!"

It was too rich a target for me to pass up. So, that night, I put together a leaflet that I'm pretty sure also ran as an art op-ed in the paper the next morning:

The Boston University Liberation Front
in association with
the ever-vigilant leaders of the People's Republic
of North Korea
cordially invite you to
Strike BU!
Smash the state, and be home by eight!
Schedule of events, subject to change:
9-ish: Meet for coffee at the Student Union
10:30: Liberate the president's office
and issue the usual nonnegotiable demands
1:00: Lunch

The demonstrators didn't succeed in shutting down the school, but later that night, angered by my leaflet, a few of them showed up outside the *Daily Free Press* offices.

When the editor and I went out to investigate, we found them waving around a bamboo pole with a noose hung around a pillow with my name on it. They called me a "running-dog lackey and braying dupe of the crypto-fascist corporate state."

The editor suggested they might want to write this in a letter to the paper. I thought their words were funnier than my leaflet.

Here's the thing: Nobody believes America is perfect. The different issues and the different struggles we face are all real. But when everything—and we do mean *everything*, from Halloween costumes to Taco Night—evokes DEFCON 1 thermonuclear outrage, sooner or later somebody's going to call you out on it, and dismiss you and all your concerns as ridiculous.

And that's what's happening right now in America.

Welcome to Snowflake U!

Trigger warning: The following letter contains educational concepts that you may find upsetting, including punctuation, spelling, and grammar whose so-called "rules" were imposed on us by the tyrannical and patriarchal canon of Western literature and philosophy.

Office of the President
September 1, 2017
Snowflake University
1 Diversity Drive
Grumble, OH 44301

Dear students:

Welcome back to another fabulous year at Snowflake U, home of the free, the brave, the gloriously self-righteous, and the permanently aggrieved!

Following up on last year's groundbreaking "Listen Up, Jackass," student-led faculty reeducation day, we're actioning on *all* your thoughtful suggestions and helpful threats.

For starters, we're adopting the new gender-neutral pronoun system instituted by Stanford. It's not just *he, she, they, Ms., Mr.,* or *Mrs.* anymore. It's *Ze, Zir, and Hirs!** We are also offering you a choice of *thirty-one* different gender identities, including bi-gender, two-spirit, pangender, pre-op, third sex, butch, and person of transgendered experience. And to answer the question from the student who's already written in wondering if he can be addressed as "Sir Dark Lord Sith Vader O'Donahue-Schwartz," we say, "Yes, Zir!"

Next, we've agreed to embrace the new no-men policy recently put into effect at Princeton, and totally eliminate the word *man* from our campus. No more *fireman,*

---

* You think we're kidding? We're not. Stanford announced the policy on August 25, 2016.

policeman, *chairman*, or *foreman*; no more *mankind*, *manpower*, *man-made*, or "Quick! Call the handyman!" It's all about the person, people!*

Like so many institutions of higher learning around the country these days, we've come to realize that the ancient white men whose names adorn the buildings on our campuses were either sexist, homophobic, or rapacious monopolistic child-employing robber barons. We considered dropping the names and assigning sequential numbers to all the buildings across campus—until we realized that *1* might be interpreted as an endorsement of American imperialism, *2* could be seen as an affirmation of conventional marriage, and *3* would almost certainly be construed as a confirmation of the Holy Trinity, the Father, Son, and Holy Ghost. So, we're going with random numbers. Try it out for yourself: "Meet me at 227, 219, 284.28."†

Taking the suggestion of some students in the Yale English Department to heart, we've decided to "decolonize" the department by dropping all the dead white writers altogether. No more Shakespeare, Dickens, Chaucer, or T. S. Eliot. They may have given us our language, but of course they were only able to do it because of white privilege.‡

On the subject of dropping things, we've heard your complaints about the grading system—so judgmental!—and the terrible injustice of "grading inequality." Particularly among students who've dropped classes in

---

* Again, we're not kidding. Princeton put this policy into effect on August 18, 2016.

† Yet again, we're not kidding. Georgetown, Duke, Princeton, Yale, Harvard, the University of North Carolina, Clemson, and the University of Mississippi are among the many schools that have been forced to address this issue. Some changed building names; others didn't.

‡ We're still not kidding. The Yale students started a petition for this in June 2016.

order to pursue "excellence in outside activism." As a result, they may have achieved average grades.[*] Let me be clear: No student at Snowflake U is "average," at anything! You are all exceptional in your own way.

Solutionizing this, our first stratagem was to institute a pass/fail system. But this raised the awful specter of a student being stigmatized by the word *fail*.

So, starting this semester, we're going with a simplified, self-esteem-enhancing pass/pass system. It's *all* good.

We applaud similar efforts at other schools, such as the University of Iowa's plan to award a bachelor's degree in social justice,[†] but we can't help but feel that word *bachelor* is sexist. And let's not get started on the word *master's*. From now on you'll receive a "degree in social awareness." I'm sure it's something your parents will cherish.

At Snowflake, we believe in the ideals of free speech, and the uncensored exchange of discomfiting ideas— up to a point. So, this year, we're moving our Outside Speakers Series into the Theater Department. We're calling the program Political Correctness Dinner Theater. We'll invite a controversial speaker, you'll protest, and we'll cancel the invitation. You get to claim victory, and we get some press. Another win-win![‡]

Beyond this, effective immediately, the History Department (or, Her-Story Department, as some of you prefer) will be rechristened—Oops! I mean *renamed*— the Oppressed People's Studies in Blame Department. Or "blame-ology," for short.

Finally, we've heard your complaints—along with the

---

[*] Sigh. Actual complaints, at Oberlin and Brown.

[†] Yup. They made this announcement on September 7, 2016.

[‡] For a full list of the schools and speakers, see the "Disinvitation Database" at the website for FIRE, the Foundation for Individual Rights in Education, at https://www.thefire.org/?s=Disinvitation+Database.

protests of students at Villanova and Portland State—
about campus security officers carrying firearms.* So
we're pulling their guns. Starting today, officers will now
engage any alleged wrongdoer in a respectful discussion
to ascertain why a questionable act took place—and
then initiate a thorough investigation to find the "root
causes" for said act, and gather evidence in order to
place the proper blame on someone else.

So, that's it! Please feel free to drop by my office anytime, for a chat, a chai tea latte, or a demand that I resign.

May all your spaces be safe spaces.

Yours, in solidarity,

Jason

Jason Pomeranian-Schultz
President, Snowflake U
(formerly known as Thomas Jefferson University)

PS: If you haven't done so already, please make sure
your parents have sent in a check for $72,000 to cover
tuition and board, by next Tuesday at the latest.

PPS: Be sure to download our new Snow Blower app,
from the Apple or Android store. It combines the best of
the MicroReport microaggression tracking app from
the University of California at Santa Cruz, with the
Islamophobia Reporting app from UC Berkeley. If anything, or anyone, offends you in any way, anywhere on
campus, just punch in the geographic coordinates, and
your Campus Action Team™ will respond immediately![†]

---

* Don't you just love Google? The protests at Villanova and Portland State
took place in September and October 2015.

† One last time: We're not making this up. UC Santa Cruz introduced its
MicroReport app in the fall of 2015, and UC Berkeley released its
Islamophobia Reporting app in August, 2016.

Working It Out

The best piece of Old School job advice O'Reilly ever received is this: "Show up early to work as much as you can."

Sends a positive message to your superiors, and separates you from the pack.

O'Reilly has worked for money since he was ten years old. That began after his father acquired a power lawn mower in 1959, allowing him to cut lawns in Levittown for $2.50 a pop.

Sounds easy. It wasn't.

Most fathers in the neighborhood, including mine, saw money as a sacred object. Parting with said object was painful and required an emotional commitment. We never had an ashtray in my house that read, "Cape Cod."

Deprivation during the Great Depression and, later, World War

II, scarred the Greatest Generation deeply. They were not about to casually hand over the meager cash they had.

Larry Larkin (last named changed), who lived on the corner of my block, had a bit more money than most. So, he hired me to cut his lawn. I showed up, cross-cut the grass, raked, and swept. His place looked excellent.

When I knocked on his door for payment, Larry, wearing a sleeveless undershirt, came out to inspect. He slowly walked around the yard, looking closely at the shortened grass blades.

Suddenly, he approached a thick bush, knelt down, lifted up the foliage, and saw some uncut grass *underneath* the shrub, completely invisible to anything but ground worms.

"You missed this," Larry said.

"Uh, Mr. Larkin, the underbrush might damage the mower, and my dad would kill me."

Whereupon Larry walked into his carport, returned with hand shears, and gave them to me. I cut the brush.

Even at age ten, I absorbed the lesson: if someone is paying you, there is a good chance pain will be inflicted.

Later that night, I told my father what had happened. He listened and summed it up.

"Larry Larkin is an imbecile."

Another pithy Old School observation.

* * *

Here is O'Reilly's job résumé: counter guy at a Carvel ice-cream store, water safety instructor teaching little kids to swim, house painter, cab driver, high school teacher, TV reporter and anchor.

Early on, I learned that my strengths lay in working hard. My

weakness was in taking orders from imbeciles, as my late father would have put it.

Because America is the land of opportunity, I quickly tired of the hourly wage deal and, at age twenty, started a painting business in Levittown. The small houses were mostly shingle with wood trim. Easy to paint unless you use oil-based paint, which we refused to do.

Remembering *Tom Sawyer*, I put together a crew to knock the houses out fast. Because we charged far less than the pros, we had to do volume.

The members of my gang all had nicknames, standard for the New York City area. We had the Bear, the Bug, Tortillo (who looked Mexican), and the Birdman. The Bear and I were partners; we paid the other guys four bucks an hour off the books. Big money in the summer of 1970.

The Bear was a stocky guy and a monster worker. I was the brains. I would talk the home owners into hiring us by pointing out that one more winter without fresh paint and caulk, and they'd be killed in their beds by a collapsing house. We had plenty of work and made lots of cash, which I kept in a big shoebox under my bed.

Running a small business taught me two Old School values: organization and execution. The crew had to show up, and they had to do their work. No wiggle room if they wanted to get paid. We literally pulled some guys out of bed early in the mornings as their moms cheered us on.

Telling the Old School truth, I was a mediocre painter but a genius at fixing problems.

One very hot day, we forgot to put a drop cloth over some bushes lining the front of a nice house. Presto, the Bug dropped his paint tray and white "Sears Best" splashed all over the greenery. Since snow was a long way off, there was nowhere to run. Not a good situation; shrubs weren't cheap.

So, while curses flew, I figured out a plan. Quickly, I threw a tarp over the now-gleaming white bushes and we resumed painting.

At quitting time, I ordered that the tarp be left in place. That night, shortly before eleven, I sneaked back to the house with a hatchet and cut the bushes down. I covered the stumps with dirt.

The next day, my crew questioned my sanity but finished the job and fled, leaving me to collect our pay from the home owner. As he and I walked around the house, he pointed out a few mistakes that were easily fixed.

Upon paying me the next day, he said, "Somehow things look different."

I deftly answered, "That's what everybody says when they get a great new paint job."

Sure.

The cash was placed into my calloused hand, and with a brief wave, I drove away.

Now, a true Old School person would have owned up to the mistake and reimbursed the owner for the cost of the bushes. But I was not Old School back then. I was more reform school. The house looked okay, and apparently nobody missed the slain bushes but the Japanese beetles.

* * *

My early career in television was a fast-paced race to make it to New York City, the nation's largest market. After graduating from Boston University with a master's degree in broadcast journalism, I got to Gotham in five years and did it the hard way: I worked my butt off.

From being the consumer reporter in Scranton, Pennsylvania, to investigating the CIA's connection to the Kennedy assassination in Dallas, to exposing cocaine trafficking in Aspen, Colorado, I was

Head shot shortly after BU graduation

a dervish of activity. I chased people down the street, told timid news executives to stuff it, and alienated about half my coworkers.

The other half liked me. So did the audiences. I was amusing, to say the least. My Old School upbringing demanded that I play no corporate games. No butt-kissing in Levittown. Hurt me in the short term, put me over the top in the long game.

I had a big advantage in climbing the TV news ladder: I stayed single. I did not have financial obligations to anyone. So, if a news-room boss was abusive or stupid (not a rare thing), I could move to another situation—which I did. Ten moves in fifteen years. I learned from every one of them.

But there was one Old School component to my performance everywhere I worked: my employers all got their money's worth from me. I never jaked it. Was I their favored son? No. Did I get them viewers? You betcha, Sarah Palin.

Life in a capitalistic marketplace is not easy. You must learn, compete, and achieve. Old School hard work is the key. Snowflake talk by the likes of Bernie Sanders about "income inequality" will hold you back. If you think that following old Bernie will ever bring you success in any way, there's an un-air-conditioned apartment in Havana I'd like to show you.

Summing up: Larry Larkin busted my chops over $2.50. But it made me stronger. Tough, hard, Old School effort always does.

You're up, Feirstein. Keep it pithy.

* * *

When you think of Old School icons, James Bond has to be at the top of the list. And it was a writer that put him there: Ian Fleming.

But in the movies, it was screenwriters who infused Bond with his Old School attitude and wit.

I was one of those writers.*

So, how do you get to write James Bond movies?

The short answer is that you start by writing a screenplay. Not a Bond script, but a screenplay that shows you can write. There's no way around this. You knock out a 105-page script with a hero and a villain, and you pray that it sells. And if it doesn't—in fact, *especially* if it doesn't—you write another. And another one after that.

That's the short answer.

The longer answer as to how I ended up living in London,

---

* I worked on *GoldenEye* (1995), *Tomorrow Never Dies* (1997), and *The World Is Not Enough* (1999).

typing the words "I've been expecting you, Mr. Bond," is more complicated, and starts back in New Jersey.*

* * *

Fade in: Newark Airport.

I had gotten it into my head that I wanted to work at Newark Airport during the summer before college. A shrink would probably say this was about some deep-seated desire to get out of Maplewood. And she probably wouldn't be entirely wrong. But I'd argue that it was also about the need to find something deep in the bottom of my pants pockets other than lint.

When I cold-called the Port Authority employment office, the outfit that runs the airport, a guy told me there was summer job program in the maintenance department. But he wasn't encouraging about my prospects. I didn't know anybody who worked at the airport; I had no connections.

"Call me back in a few weeks," he said dismissively, clearly hoping he'd never hear from me again.

For three months, I called every Monday at four thirty until he finally gave me the job. I thought I'd scored a victory and that the hard part was over. I was wrong.

Standing outside a 1930s airplane hangar that had been turned into a maintenance garage, about twenty of us listened as the foreman read off our names from a clipboard on the first morning of

---

* FYI: If you're planning to tackle a screenplay, you've got to tell the story in three acts: First, you get someone up a tree, then you throw stones at him, and then you get him down. It's the structure used in almost every movie you've ever seen: Boy meets girl, boy loses girl, boy gets girl. Or, as John Ford, the director of John Wayne's *The Searchers*, described all his Westerns: A man rides into town. The man cleans up the town. The man rides out. All Ford left out was a little explanation of the middle bit, the second act, after the guy rides into town, which can also be summarized as "mayhem ensues."

work. The boss was a short guy in his mid-forties with the physique of a floor safe. Half the kids came from an inner-city jobs program; the rest were the sons of firemen, policemen, and jet fuel tanker drivers. There were no girls. We all wore dark-green Port Authority work uniforms.

After reading off my name, the boss paused. He looked over at me, cocking his head and narrowing his eyes. "You're from Maplewood?"

"Yes," I said helpfully.

He frowned and continued reading out names. And from that moment on, I didn't need to be an air traffic controller to know that he wanted me out of the airport. For the next six weeks, whatever crummy, miserable, awful job came up was mine.

Putrid food needed to be cleaned out of a freezer where it'd been rotting for a year after the electricity was turned off in a bankrupt terminal restaurant?

"Let Maplewood do it."

Sledgehammering blunt rebar rods through six inches of cement to install tire stops in a parking lot?

"Hand Maplewood the sledge."

Week by week, the tension between us grew. Things finally came to a head in August, when he drove me out to the far end of the airport one morning and told me to dig holes "twenty feet apart" for a new fence at the end of a runway. Then he drove off, leaving me to dig holes in the ninety-five-degree heat while I watched cranes work on the twin towers rising in Lower Manhattan, a few miles away.

At three thirty that afternoon, he returned in an orange pickup truck whose bed was filled with fence posts and a crew of summer hires.

"Sorry. I forgot to pick you up for lunch," he said, bounding out of the truck with a nasty smile. He pointed to the holes I'd dug, telling the crew, "Use every other one."

He saw me bristle. I saw his jaw clench. The other kids stepped back, anticipating a fistfight. The boss looked at me sharply.

"You got a problem with that, Maplewood?"

Eleven years later, I'd see almost this exact scene play out between Louis Gossett Jr. and Richard Gere in *An Officer and a Gentleman*. And just like Gere's character, Zack Mayo, I couldn't quit. I needed the money. I had nowhere else to go. So, I swallowed my pride and backed off.

"No, I've got no problem at all," I said, and went to work putting in fence posts and filling in half the holes I'd spent the day digging in the hot sun.

Now, the thing of it is if you'd asked me back then, at that moment, why the boss was treating me sadistically, I would've probably rolled out a list of things, starting with my religion. But now I see it differently. If screenwriting teaches you anything, it's that in order for a scene to work, and ring true, you have to take what you've written and replay it from every character's point of view: Does it make sense that he would say this? Would the character really act this way?

Replaying that summer now, I wonder if when the boss looked at me that first morning, what he actually saw was a long-haired punk who still hadn't lost his baby fat, had never worked a hard day in his life, and needed to be toughened up.

Two Old School rules: Never, ever give up. And never ascribe the worst motives to someone when there might be a much simpler reason for their behavior.

Sometimes, people can just be jerks.

* * *

Dissolve to: Miami Beach, Florida. August 1972

The scene is the Republican National Convention. The Nixon campaign is holed up in the Doral Hotel, which has been turned into a fortress. Outside, a wheelchair-bound Vietnam vet named Ron Kovic is leading a thousand demonstrators up Collins Avenue, protesting the war. I'm working as an intern for United Press International, trying to maneuver a red Cadillac Eldorado filled with UPI reporters past the steel wall of buses encircling the Miami Beach Convention Center. Later, I'll be ripping copy from Teletype machines on the midnight-to-eight shift at our headquarters in the garage at the Fontainebleau Hotel.

How did *this* come to pass?

Connections.

At the Boston University college newspaper, our managing editor, Martha Battenfeld, had a brother who worked for UPI. She made the introduction.

Down at the Miami convention hall, all the interns were awestruck by the sight of Walter Cronkite, John Chancellor, and Norman Mailer. The three of them cruised through the convention floor like ocean liners, with their assistants bobbing and weaving to clear the way. We wanted to be part of it. But how? Realizing we were the only "longhairs" working for UPI, we lobbied to cover the protestors' encampment at Flamingo Park. We got the assignment.

I wrote a story about watching the Yippie leaders Abbie Hoffman and Jerry Rubin in the carnival-like atmosphere at "People's Park," as the site was being called, but UPI turned it down. It was my first rejection—and surely not the last.

Old School lesson: Don't take rejection personally. The editors were right. My writing wasn't ready for prime time.

* * *

Cut to Boston, summer 1973.

I've gotten a part-time job at a small computer typesetting shop in Brookline, a suburb of Boston, putting together "community shopper" newspapers. I'm earning $2.50 an hour, around $25.00 a week. It seems like good money at the time—until, that is, the union that represents linotype machine operators comes in and promises us *$12.50 an hour* if we organize and become a union shop. If the owners refuse to sign the union contract, we'll go on strike!

This evokes the oldest of all Old School rules: if something sounds too good to be true, it probably is.

We went on strike. Then the owners closed the business. I lost my job. Ultimately, though it would take years to play out, the union failed at what the owners argued was its actual motive: stopping computer typesetting from making the linotype operators' jobs obsolete.

* * *

Cut to Newbury Street, Boston, April 1974.

One night, I passed a white billboard whose upper edge had been scalloped to look like a snowbank, with the words "Ski Me" written in large type and, underneath, in smaller type, a line about visiting Maine's ski resorts.

I thought it was smart and witty. I learned that it had been created by Steve Cosmopulos, a zany genius who cofounded an advertising agency that also did political campaigns. One of Steve's quirks was that he started work at 6:00 a.m.

Hoping to get an internship, I sent Cosmopulos a letter and included some of the ads and columns I'd written. In what seemed like less time than it takes for the postage stamps to dry, he sent back a funny handwritten note. (A very Old School move, by the way, one that also applies to e-mail: pay someone the courtesy of answering promptly.) He told me to call and make an appointment to see him.

So, I did—at 6:00 in the morning, which he found amusing and, for which, immediately started to tease me.

"Shouldn't you be *sleeping*?" he asked. "Aren't you in *college*?"

Before I could answer, he heard a car horn blare on my end of the call.

Perplexed, he hesitated. "Wait a minute. Where *are* you?"

"Downstairs. Across the street from your building."

Cosmopulos laughed. "That's a first. Nobody's ever done *that* before. I'll be right down to open the door."

When Steve offered me an internship, and a summer job, that morning, I jumped at it. I ended up writing ads for the mayor's office and for a politician whose arrival took all of us by surprise: Bob Dole, the Republican senator from Kansas, who was in a tight reelection race in the aftermath of Watergate.

But here's the kicker: On my first day of work, Steve introduced me to an art director. The guy looked me over, nodded his approval, and asked, "So, what is he? A writer or an art director?"

"He's a *writer*," Steve replied. And with that sentence, he changed my life forever. Instinctively, he knew what I really wanted to do.

I could never repay Steve for taking me under his wing. Somewhere, we all have somebody like that, someone who gave us a break, little or large, out of the generosity in his heart. *So, pay it forward.* You pay back the person who gave you a break by paying it forward, helping some other young person find his way, even if he doesn't know where he's going yet.

* * *

Cut to New York 1979.

After graduating from BU, I spent the next few years working as an advertising copywriter in Manhattan. I wrote ads for political candidates and consumer products like BMW and Sony. But I felt like I was missing out on something. It was the era of *National Lampoon* and *Saturday Night Live*. I wanted to write the funny stuff, not the ads in between.

An advertising buddy, Frank Schwartz, and I began writing a screenplay. We'd leave our jobs at six and write every night till midnight. Weekends, too. And when I wasn't working on the script, I started submitting "humor" pieces to magazines.

After eight months, our script was done. What happened next was a coincidence so bizarre that I wouldn't believe it if I saw it in a movie: A young editor at *Glamour*, Katy Dobbs, published one my pieces. Her boyfriend worked for Barry Diller, the CEO of Paramount Pictures. A few weeks later, Frank and I were in Los Angeles, sitting in an executive's office on the Paramount lot, getting notes about how to improve our script. Paramount executive Jeffrey Katzenberg wasn't happy with our rewrite, so he replaced us with two writers from SCTV. But then he wasn't happy with *their* rewrite of *our* rewrite, so he brought us back to LA to work with a director who'd been hired to supervise the next draft.

So far, none of this is unusual. It's the way the movie business works.

We met the director in his office on Sunset Boulevard at nine o'clock on a Monday morning. He was a big hairy guy with a New Yawk accent who could probably have been cast on the TV show *Grizzly Adams*—as one of the bears.

The Bear was sitting on a leather couch with two piles of scripts on the coffee table in front of him: ours and the draft from the SCTV guys.

He bit into his breakfast: a raw tomato. "So, which script would *you* make?" he demanded, spitting tomato seeds all over the office.

Frank gave me a look: *You* take this, his eyes said.

I took a deep breath. "Actually, I think we should work from our script," I answered. "It's the one the studio bought."

The Bear exploded. "F—k you!" he bellowed, jumping to his feet. "Get the f— out of my office. I'm not gonna work with anybody who's in love with his own words!"

By now, Frank was also on his feet. "No! No!" he cried, "Bruce didn't mean it! We'll do whatever you want! We just want to make this work!"

The Bear looked sidewise at Frank. "F—k you, too," he said. "I'm not going to work with anyone who won't stand up for what he believes in."

And with that, he turned and bolted from the room.

Frank and I looked at each other, stunned and utterly speechless. We would find out only later was really going on: the Bear wanted to break his contract with Paramount. When he left the office, he drove across town to start work on another picture, at Fox.

Tragically, Frank died of a heart attack a few years later. Not a day goes by that I don't think about him.

But on that morning, in that office, he just looked at me with a wry smile and a shrug and said, "Welcome to Hollywood."*

---

* The script was called *High Finance*. It was the story of a ne'er-do-well young banker (think Tim Matheson in *Animal House*) who has screwed up on some bad real estate loans and decided to save his job by convincing a crazy Latin American dictator to let the bank invest in his marijuana business. While he's in South America, he meets a Mafia princess who has convinced her father that it's time to let "a girl" take her rightful place in the business by renegotiating their deal with the dictator. In the screenplay, hilarity and romance ensue. In real life, the picture never got made.

* * *

Every so often you read about somebody who says that working in Hollywood is like going to war. It's ridiculous. That's way out of line.

Getting paid money, real money, to make stuff up is nothing short of a miracle. And walking onto a sound stage where the cast and crew are buzzing around a set that *you've* imagined is both literally, and figuratively, a dream come true.

Still, screenwriting is a nasty business. Everybody's got "notes" on your writing; you can get fired in an instant; most of what you write will never get made. And sooner or later, the paychecks dwindle, and the studios stop calling.

In other words, it's fun until it isn't.

The average length of a screenwriter's career is about ten years. And after five years in Hollywood, I'd had enough.

I was burnt out.

I'd taken too many idiotic notes from studio executives.[*] I'd even heard a producer scream at me over the phone, "I hope you get cancer and die."

I'd grown weary of what I perceived to be the basic social contract in Hollywood: All relationships are transactional. Meaning, we agree to be friends, so long as we can help each other.

And I'd still rather forget the New Year's Eve party at which a

---

[*] My favorite example of this is the note I got on a screenplay about a singles bar in Manhattan: Sitting in a restaurant, our star is complaining to his best friend about his awful dating life. When the waiter serves lunch, the best friend points to his pal's plate and says, "That's your problem. *Real men don't eat quiche.*" A producer circled this line in red ink, writing, "This is what's wrong with the screenplay. It's not funny." Out of pure spite, I turned the line into a book . . . whereupon the producer started taking credit for giving me the idea!

famous actress and I flirted with each other across a candlelit dinner table. Let's call her Lucy.

Sometime very late in the night, after many too many bottles of champagne, I turned to her slightly drunk best friend, sitting next to me, and said, "You know, Lucy really is cute."

At which point, the best friend instantly sobered up. "Don't even think about it."

"Why not?" I asked.

"Because you're nobody."

* * *

So, I moved back to New York.

I started writing for Graydon Carter and Kurt Andersen at *Spy* magazine. I moved with Carter to write a column for the *New York Observer*, which led to a stint writing unsigned editorials for the *New York Times*. And after being named editor in chief of *Vanity Fair*, Graydon invited me to rejoin him, where I've been ever since.

Old School credo: Stay loyal to the people who are good to you. You'll earn their loyalty in return.

Through all this, I still loved movies. And I still wrote screenplays, but not for the studios. And in another one of those "you couldn't make this up" coincidences, a script I'd written about prohibition-era gangsters in Newark caught the attention of the Broadway and film producer Fred Zollo, who shared it with his then-girlfriend, Barbara Broccoli, whose father, Cubby Broccoli, produced the Bond films. In turn, she shared it with her stepbrother, and coproducer of the Bond films, Michael Wilson.

Then I got the call from Barbara and Michael. Would I like to spend three weeks in London tweaking the dialogue on *Golden-Eye*?

Three weeks turned into five years, and three Bond films that I either wrote or cowrote with other screenwriters. Then, six Bond video games in the decade that followed.*

Viewed from the outside, this may seem like a lot of luck and coincidence. There's no denying they both played a role.

But I'll share something the actor William Hurt said about show business careers: "You've got to be good enough, to get lucky enough, to *get* good enough, to be lucky enough to do the things you love."

It's the actor's version of O'Reilly's Old School: "Show up early to work as much as you can." The luck will follow.

---

* If you're wondering how somebody goes from writing romantic comedies to action movies, I'll let you in on a secret: they're not all that different. In one, you try to prevent your characters from falling in love for as long as possible; in the other, you try to delay the final showdown for as long as possible. In a romantic comedy, you put them in a kitchen and use everything in the room (food, knives, microwave ovens) to keep them apart; in an action movie, you use all the same items to have them try to kill each other.

A Guide to Old School Businesses vs. Snowflake Businesses

	OLD SCHOOL	SNOWFLAKE
Company name	Something that gives *some* indication of what the company actually does (i.e., US Steel)	An opaque amalgam of words and phrase that give no indication as to what the company actually does (i.e., Tronc)
Most powerful person in the company?	The CEO	The head of Human Resources
What does the company actually do?	Make stuff	Disrupt . . . something while changing the paradigm . . . with cutting-edge technologies
Can you be a little more specific?	Manufacturing	Um . . . something that involves a lot of social media
Typical job title	Vice president of engineering	Grand pooh-bah for inspiration
Dress code	Suits, dresses, business attire	Hoodies and flip-flops
Business accessories	Briefcases	Backpacks
Vacation policy	Depends on how long you've been at the company	You say you want to go to Coachella or Burning Man? Sure!
Typical business correspondence salutation	Dear Mr./Mrs./Ms./ Sir/Madame	Yo! Hey! Bro! Dude! Dude-ess!
What position do you aspire to?	C-suite corner office	Head of social media
Lunch policy	There is no free lunch.	Where's my free lunch? Vegan Tuesdays.
Key buzzwords	*Profit, loss, customer service*	*Incentivize, strategize, pivot, personal branding*

	OLD SCHOOL	SNOWFLAKE
Dumb ideas	Outsource customer service to India	Inject progressive politics into our advertising campaigns
Diversity policy	We do our best to promote women and minorities.	We talk a lot about diversity—but don't look too closely at our numbers, please.
Has the company ever turned a profit?	Yes	No
What do employees enjoy most about their jobs?	A sense of accomplishment	Spending half the day on Facebook
If something goes wrong . . .	Deal with it internally, and never make the company look bad	Whine on social media or write a tell-all book
How do employees see themselves?	Road warriors	Social justice warriors
What can you expect at the end of the year?	Bonuses	Pink slips

The Old School Blues

It was the Summer of Love, but O'Reilly was not involved. The year was 1967. High school graduation came and went without incident, and it was time to make some summer money teaching little kids to swim and making sure no one drowned in a fairly busy Long Island pool.

But someone almost did.

One morning, I was strolling around the pool twirling my whistle when I looked down in the ten-foot deep end and saw an unusual thing: an urchin was on the bottom of the pool looking up. He did not look happy.

Immediately, I jumped in the water, swam down, hooked the kid across the chest, and brought him up to the surface. I got the boy, who was about four, out of the pool and placed him on a towel. He said nothing.

A commotion ensued, and the boy's mother came running over. She had no idea how he'd become submerged.

Even though the mom was quizzing the kid, he was having none of it. He took the Fifth: said not a word.

Anyway, the mom asked me for my name and promised to tell my boss how great I was, etcetera.

About thirty-five years later, I am signing books in a Long Island store and a man walks up to me and says, "You saved my life!" It was the kid. Once I became a national news guy, his mother apparently tracked me down and alerted her son to the book event.

Amazing story about Old School gratitude.

Now back to the Summer of Love. The rise of the Age of Aquarius was very bad news for the Old School curriculum. With the Vietnam War raging and blacks angry over lack of opportunity, dissent swept in, much of it reasonable.

Quickly, social mores changed. Drugs, especially marijuana, became cool and acceptable. Millions of Americans grew their hair very long. As Kid Rock later sang, "My thoughts were short, my hair was long."

Sex without commitment was suddenly available. The Old School way of looking at life was battered by the hippie mantra of sex, drugs, and rock and roll. As Dylan sang, the times they were a changin'.

In January 1967, the Rolling Stones were booked on *The Ed Sullivan Show* to sing their hit "Let's Spend the Night Together." Old School guy Ed demanded that the band change the lyrics "the night" to "some time," which they did. I remember watching that program and was fascinated by the band's cofounder, Brian Jones, his bangs hanging so low they threatened to cover his mouth. Even at a somewhat naïve seventeen, I knew Jones was stoned, pardon the pun.

The troubled Brian Jones wound up dead at the bottom of his pool. He was twenty-seven.

Later in '67, the Doors showed up on Ed's show. This time the cranky host told lead singer Jim Morrison to change the phrase "girl we couldn't get much higher," from the song "Light My Fire." Apparently, Morrison agreed, but then sang the original words with a smirk bigger than the one Jones had had. Sullivan went ballistic and banned the Doors from appearing on his show again.

The charismatic Jim Morrison was found dead in a bathtub in 1971. He was also twenty-seven.

All summer long, chaos simmered. There were race riots, antiwar protests, subversive television. The Smothers Brothers mocked their country on CBS, the *Laugh-In* crew cut a pilot for NBC.

The Old School belief system was getting hammered everywhere. Bitterness, not patriotism, was the order of the day. Restraint and moderation were laughed at. Confusion reigned as country, church, and convention were all redefined in negative ways.

It would be wrong to call the young protesters Snowflakes, just as it would be grossly unfair to blame Old School adherents for America's societal crisis. The two sides were very angry with each other, but neither held the higher moral ground.

The historical truth is that the Vietnam War began with President Kennedy's noble intention of keeping the South Vietnamese people free from communism, which dominated North Vietnam. Under President Harry Truman, the United States countered the Communist North Koreans, thereby ensuring freedom for millions of people in the south of that country. JFK wanted the same for South Vietnam.

But the mid-1960s were a long way from the early 1950s, and Vietnam was a far different place from Korea. For starters, the World War II attitude that one's country was owed unquestioned allegiance by its citizens was still dominant during the Korean campaign. By the mid-1960s, though, that sentiment had evaporated, and many young Americans had no desire to be drafted and sent halfway around the world to fight in a steaming hot jungle.

As antiwar mania rose, Old School disciples bristled. The clash of cultures sometimes even fractured families. The social civil war in America was incredibly intense.

In Levittown, where many World War II vets were raising families, there was mostly sadness. The guys who didn't get college deferments shipped out. Many came home different people. One guy I knew committed suicide; two others were drug addicts. Even though Old School values were still in place in my working-class neighborhood, most of us knew that Vietnam was a hellish place. We didn't need Walter Cronkite to tell us that—the changes we saw in our Vietnam vet friends said it all.

My father knew the score. My cousin Dickie Melton walked point in the jungles of Vietnam with a scout dog. He and my father commiserated. Both men spared me the details, but my father never bad-mouthed the protesters and had no use for President Lyndon Johnson.

Preparing for college in 1967, I concentrated on making money and getting in shape for football. I knew that hippies were running wild in San Francisco listening to Jimi Hendrix singing "Purple Haze," but that was a faraway scene that did not directly affect me.

By the way, a few years later, Hendrix was found dead in a London flat. You guessed it, he was twenty-seven.

Because nothing changed in my house, my Old School upbringing protected me as the Age of Excess blew in with a whoosh that knocked down many of my peers. I wasn't eager to try drugs or hang with the flag burners. My traditional beliefs placed barriers between me and risky behavior. I was far more restrained in my actions than many of my friends, who went absolutely wild. I really had no desire to feel groovy or engage in "far-out" behavior, even if Janis Joplin was.

Again, you guessed it, Janis died in a seedy Los Angeles hotel at age twenty-seven.

Four major rock stars dead before their twenty-eighth birthday. Old School values could have saved them.

My only shot at love during the summer of '67 was ruined by my Old School posture. A very pretty girl took me to a party and, on the way, casually told me that her parents were away for the weekend. It took me a few minutes, but I figured it out.

Anyway, we show up at a nice suburban house, and music is blaring. Iron Butterfly or something. Maybe Vanilla Fudge.* We walk through the front door into a mushroom cloud of pot smoke. Zoned-out teens everywhere. Almost immediately the girl locates some friends who offer her a marijuana cigarette. She takes it and then tries to hand it to me. I decline. Stares. Party pooper.

I leave; she stays.

Where have you gone Alice B. Toklas?†

Old School values actually saved me from the sixties. Addiction runs in my family—my maternal grandfather and a first cousin were heavy drinkers. But I never wavered, never hurt myself or anyone else while inebriated, because I've never been inebriated. In college, while many students were walking zombies, I stayed sober, accomplishing a lot and setting the table for a successful career.

---

* Iron Butterfly and Vanilla Fudge were heavy metal rock bands who had hits in the late 1960s. A few of them managed to survive with enough of their hearing intact to still be touring in 2017.

† *I Love You, Alice B. Toklas* was a 1968 comedy starring Peter Sellers. The title is a reference to the partner of Gertrude Stein, Alice B. Toklas, who wrote a popular cookbook featuring pot brownie recipes.

*After the turmoil of the 1960s, we ended up with disco
and the Bee Gees?*

The counterculture madness ran out of steam after the war
ended and the mid-seventies arrived. Looking back, most Old School
traditions survived, but just barely.

Then came the blowback. When the Age of Aquarius finally
subsided, it was replaced by another frenzied era: disco! Talk about
an amazing transition. Good-bye, Crosby, Stills and Nash. Hello,
Bee Gees!

Summing up: Old School was out for a few turbulent years, and
many paid a steep price for it. Now, however, traditions are respected
in many quarters—a good thing. The fight, however, continues in

this age of celebrated secularism, where personal gratification is the ultimate accomplishment.

Indeed, there may be danger up ahead as cyberspace changes everything. How that will affect Old School will soon be discussed.

First, though, Feirstein is going to tell us something about his counterculture experience.

* * *

I played in a rock band. I wore the fringe jacket. I had the long hair. I thought it was a great way to meet girls. But instead of getting groupies, what I actually got was partial hearing loss. This is why I sometimes wonder if instead of being known as the Me Generation or the Baby Boomers, perhaps we'd be more accurately described as the What? Generation—as in "What did you say? Can you repeat that?"

They say that if you remember the sixties, you probably weren't there.*

The observation resonates with us because it's all-too-accurate for the group of people who went down the road of drugs and, in one way or another, never came back.

That wasn't me. I didn't go down that road.

I still remember the smell of smoke from Newark burning. I remember the store where I bought my first guitar, looted and smoldering. I remember the music, the war, the assassinations of Martin Luther King Jr. and Bobby Kennedy. I remember the long, slow black train carrying Bobby Kennedy's body from Washington, DC, to New York, as it passed through Newark's Penn Station.

---

* On the Internet, this is wrongly credited to Robin Williams or the Jefferson Airplane's Grace Slick or Paul Kantner. (I'm shocked! I'm stunned! The Internet gets something wrong?) But it was actually first said by the comedian Charles Fleisher, in 1982.

From the duck-and-cover nuclear bomb drills in grammar school, to JFK in Dallas, to RFK and Martin Luther King Jr. in 1968, I thought this was the way America worked. The abnormal seemed normal. But none of it was as personal, or came so close to home, as the war in Vietnam.

In my house, as in so many others, the lyrics from Stephen Stills's Buffalo Springfield classic "For What It's Worth" were all too real: There were "battle lines being drawn" across the dinner table, every night. I had a cousin in Saigon, an uncle in the Air Force Reserve, and a father who kept his World War II medals in blue leather boxes in the top drawer of his bedroom dresser.

One night, after yet another meal of silence and spaghetti, my father announced, "We're not going to fight about this anymore. I want you to go for draft counseling."

I knew that he was issuing an order. He was expecting that I'd get some sage advice about college deferments and which branch of the service I should join: the army, the navy, or the air force.

So, the next day, I went over to Seton Hall University, in South Orange, New Jersey, got the "draft counseling," and returned home to issue my report that night.

"What did they tell you?" my father asked.

"They said I could get a shrink to say I'm crazy and give me a psychological deferment," I told him. "Or we could move to Canada."

My father blinked. "We're doomed," he said.

In the weeks that followed, he changed his mind about the war, worn down by the increasingly bad news from Vietnam. And a few years after that, when it was my turn to participate in the draft lottery, my birthday came up at number 362, in a year when the cutoff number for getting called up for service barely broke the single digits.

Lucky.

* * *

The smartest historical overview of twentieth-century America I've ever read was William Manchester's *The Glory and The Dream: A Narrative History of America, 1932–1972.* The book begins in 1932 with a vignette of army chief of staff Gen. Douglas Mac-Arthur, the man in charge of what was then the sixth-largest army in the world, after Czechoslovakia's, sending his assistant, Maj. Dwight Eisenhower, to fill out the paperwork to requisition two trolley tokens, in order to travel to Capitol Hill and testify in front of Congress. The book ends forty years later, with antiwar protestors demonstrating in the streets outside the Watergate hearings.

If there's one thing you learn from Manchester's book, it's that almost everything we think is new and controversial in America has happened at least once before. The first radio demagogue was Father Charles Coughlin, in the 1930s; the original "America First" movement dates to Charles Lindbergh, in 1940. Where a small but vocal group of people wondered if America was ready for a Catholic president in 1960, a similar group wondered if we were ready for a black president in 2008.

One way or another, common sense prevails. Father Coughlin was gone from the radio by 1939; Charles Lindbergh was sidelined by the time we entered World War II. Both Kennedy and Obama were elected president. Sooner or later, we course-correct.

* * *

When O'Reilly asked me to collaborate on a book about Old School, it occurred to me that while I first heard the phrase as a child, I was suddenly hearing it again, after a long absence, in popular culture.

Recently I'd heard it while in the car stuck in traffic, on the radio, in Los Angeles. An FM station announced that it was going "old school," back to the days of Motown; Marvin Gaye; Stevie Wonder; Aretha Franklin; Earth, Wind & Fire, "When music had lyrics, and melody."

I don't want to get all metaphorical here, but I can't help but suspect that this is what so many people are looking for in their lives today.

Old School is the words and the melodies, the things that make sense.

But let me be clear: Old school is not about some old guy standing on his front porch screaming at the kids, "Get off my lawn!" Nor is it about some overly romanticized longing for the 1950s, when, the truth is, life was *not* wonderful for a lot of Americans.

Old School is about looking at the past and deciding what's worth keeping and what's better left behind.

It's looking at the present and recognizing what's worth embracing and what's ridiculous and better tossed aside.

Above all else, it's hoping you have the experience, and the wisdom, to know the difference.

Midterms

We're halfway through the book, the perfect time to test your growing Old School acumen.

1) You're a member of a large political party in America. Over the previous eight years, while one of your members sat in the White House, you lost 11 seats in the U.S. Senate, 39 seats in the House of Representatives, 958 seats in state legislatures, and 10 governor's mansions. You also lost control of 13 state legislatures, and your most recent candidate for the Oval Office was defeated by an Electoral College count of 306 to 232. What's the correct Old School response to this:

   a) recognize that if you're digging yourself into a hole, maybe it's time to stop digging, and maybe try to learn something from your losses; or

   b) change nothing, reelect your leadership, and blame the voters for being too dumb to realize what's good for them?

2) When you hear the word *victim*, what's the first thing you think of:

   a) something I saw on an episode of *NCIS* last night; or

   b) myself and my current lot in life, where I am the victim of our classist, oppressive, misanthropic society, where absolutely nothing is my fault? Can I go back to playing video games and posting on Facebook now?

3) What's the proper closing salutation for business correspondence:

   a) Sincerely yours; or

   b) CUL8R?

4) When you hear someone on television say, "It's time we had a national conversation" about something, do you:

   a) change the channel, hoping you can find the latest installment of *Sharknado*; or

b) take copious notes and engage your family, friends, and business associates in a one-sided conversation, lecturing that everything they know, think, and believe about the subject is wrong?

5) There's a power blackout. Do you:

a) shrug as you go to the drawer filled with flashlights and batteries, musing on the old proverb "It's better to light a candle than curse the darkness"; or

b) sit in the darkness, stewing about America's failure to invest in sustainable energy sources, particularly wind and solar, while cursing that your cell phone batteries are dying and you can't get on the Internet to tweet about this?

10

Tech It Out

If it's a Luddite you're looking for, you've found him.* I am hopeless on the devices, which on television I call "machines." I don't like them, don't know an app from an asp, and believe they badly damage Old School values like looking somebody in the eye and stating your case with honor.

The stupid machines are also addictive cyberspace opium. You know it, and I know it.

Yes, yes, yes, I realize you can get information instantly, say "Happy birthday" to Grandma in ten seconds, and find your spouse

---

* The word *Luddite* dates to the beginning of the industrial age in England, in 1811, when a group of textile workers (allegedly led by a weaver named Ned Ludd) destroyed the new mechanized looms at cotton mills in order to preserve their jobs. These days, it's defined as someone who is befuddled by new technology and rejects it, presumably to preserve his sanity.

without even leaving the house. I know the machines can make life easier. But the downside is *huge*, as Trump might say.

So, let's take a look.

One major deficit is that the world of machines empowers sniveling cowards who used to be shunned by decent people. These smear merchants and Morlocks (Google "H. G. Wells's *Time Machine*") can now verbally assassinate anyone while concealing their own identity. It's Defamation Alley as these lowlifes take delight in saying disgusting, revolting things about their fellow human beings while hiding behind an anonymous posture.

The result: cyberbullying has emotionally crippled millions of people. In the past, guttersnipes could be dealt with harshly because, unless they hired a plane to skywrite, you knew who they were. Now these baskets of deplorables (thank you, Hillary) can spew their hatred nonstop from their basement depots.

Awful.

Then there's privacy. We don't have any. If you use the machine, count on your transmissions going public. They will at some point. The Old School value of trust does not exist in cyberspace because immoral behavior is celebrated and dissenting voices are texted down. There is no restraint.

Then there's childhood. The more that children use their devices, the faster kiddom disappears. They can be exposed to debasement and degeneration instantly; the language and images have few limits. And if parents say no, the kids are almost ostracized because other children play incessantly on these things. No longer do many children play outside; now they interact on machines.

The result is a mass desensitizing of young people. Wait until you see how that plays out in the years to come.

And there's more. Hackers can invade your space and violate your private correspondence. Anything you transmit can be ultimately used against you. Vicious Net clowns can access your address, phone number, medical data, school history—everything! Thanks to social media sociopaths, the idea of a "private life" is obsolete.

Hackers even get people killed by exposing security secrets and military intelligence, as the WikiLeaks case demonstrates.

So, cowards now have more power than at any other time in history. They can secretly tape your words, take your picture, send your kids porn, threaten your life, send unwanted stuff to your house—the list of atrocities is endless.

Convinced yet?

The long-term effect of the high-tech revolution is just beginning to come into focus, and the influence it is having on many of us is devastating. Part of the Old School curriculum is actually setting aside time to *think*—that is, using your brain to examine your conscience, appreciate nature, solve personal problems in a responsible way, actually consider how you can help other people, and game plan for future challenges and opportunities.

Yet time for such pursuits has been obliterated by incessant texting, gaming, Facebooking, or whatever else the Net addiction requires. We are becoming a nation of Kardashians: self-absorbed zombies who could not care less about the social contract that requires compassionate attention to others.

How many times have you been in a restaurant and observed folks all around you texting instead of talking to one another? I mean, you can't even walk down the street without dodging people who have their heads down, eyes glued to the machine.

How many people have been killed in cars because drivers are using their machines behind the wheel? How many children are being ignored by their parents who choose to text rather than play with their kids?

If there was ever an assault on Old School behavior, this is it. Intense action is required to ward off the Visigoths and avoid becoming one yourself.*

So, here are some Old School rules of the road. Call them defense mechanisms, if you will.

Machine Rules

—No machines at mealtimes. Give your digestive system a break.

—No machines in bed.

—Set aside the iPhone madness for a designated time each day so you can pursue nonmachine activities like actually speaking to other human beings or walking through the woods *without* headphones.

—Read a book with paper pages from time to time.

—Watch TV without texting at the same time.

—Develop a hobby that has nothing to do with social media.

—Plan an activity more than three days in advance. One of the unintended consequences of social media is that people are so preoccupied with the texting present that they fail to think ahead.

—Don't have sex using the machine; you'll pay a price if you do.

The bold truth is that Old School alumni are the last chance to blunt the Walking Dead hordes. We have to fight the madness and reject the destructive lifestyle that social media obsession brings.

---

* The Visigoths were a fierce, marauding Germanic tribe that sacked Rome in 410 and eventually had their asses kicked by the Umayyad Muslims in 711.

Want to know why Hillary Clinton and Trump reached the top rungs in politics? Because many Americans could not have cared less about their country. They know absolutely nothing about geopolitical realities. All they knew was what their machines told them, truth be damned.

For me, an Old School guy, social media is the great white shark devouring all the attributes that lead to true success in life.

These are, in no particular order:

Old School Attributes

— Awareness of the needs of others
— The ability to distinguish right from wrong, good from evil
— The courage to promote good and to confront evil
— The ability to honestly assess your own character and that of others (you can't evaluate another person on a machine; you actually have to physically interact with someone in order to understand who he is)
— The development of a spiritual life (even if you do not believe in a creator, there are mysteries of life worth thinking about, there is a personal philosophy worth developing, but none of that will happen if you spend a large part of your life on social media)
— Believing in something beyond yourself (proclaiming loyalty to other people, your country, your faith)

One of the reasons tens of millions of children are devastated by divorce is that loyalty is no longer emphasized in America and almost completely nonexistent in cyberspace. Personal gratification is everything; there is no self-sacrifice on the Net.

You think the current heroin and opiate epidemic is an accident? It's directly related to gratification whatever the risk. Social media can be an addiction, and one addiction can easily lead to another.

If Old School values don't come back, this planet is doomed. It's just a matter of when, not if, the savages will do irreparable damage.

Sorry to be the Paul Revere of pessimism, but the machines are now so powerful that they are overwhelming those of weak character and even threatening decent people. Awareness of the problem is the first line of defense. Keeping the Old School faith is the final wall.

So, there you go.

Thank God, Feirstein is not as hysterical on the tech deal as I am, because at this point we all need some relief from me!

Come to think of it, that's a good tweet.

* * *

Don't hold back here, Bill. Tell us what you *really* think.

Assuming the smoke alarms didn't go off in your house while reading O'Reilly's rant about technology, you've got to forgive him. This is not a guy who signs off e-mails with ROFL ("rolling on the floor laughing") or little smiley faces.

As you may have noticed on TV, he's not exactly shy when it comes to expressing his opinions about the things that bother him. And there's almost nothing I've seen that presses his buttons more than the Internet and modern technology.

He is, as he's quick to point out, a simple man.

I can just imagine him at home, padding down to breakfast one morning in a bathrobe and slippers, only to discover a brand-new coffee maker that has more buttons and switches than the *Apollo 13* command module that took us to the moon.

Not a pretty picture.

Better still, picture him on the phone with computer tech support.

"You have to reboot the computer, sir."

"You mean *kick* it?"

"No, reinitialize it."

"You mean *sign* it? With a *pen?*"

"No, I mean turn it off and restart it."

"Why didn't you just say that in the first place?"

Or imagine him with a car salesman who's just finished touting 19 USB ports, 11 coffee cup holders, a rear-facing camera, a heads-up display, and a radio with 431 presets.

"So where does the key go in? How do you start it?"

"There is no key. You press this button."

Cue the O'Reilly death stare. "Are you kidding me? A button? What lunatic came up with *that?*"

Better still, imagine O'Reilly interviewing the one guy who truly encapsulates the misguided belief in the mystical powers of technology: Darth Vader.

"So, Vader, thanks for coming in to talk to us about the Death Star."

"I feel the Force within you, O'Reilly. It's powerful."

"Don't try to spin me, Vader. Let's drop the talking points. I just want to get to the bottom of this: It seems that every time you build a Death Star, somebody comes along and blows it up. A lot of people are questioning your leadership on this. A billion dollar weapons program, and you can't get it right. What say you?"

"You're challenging the Force?"

"Put away the laser saber, Vader. I'm just looking out for the folks on the Death Star here. What pinhead allowed this to happen? And what are you going to do to make sure it doesn't happen again?"

"You're a stand-up guy, Vader."

"I can't get into specifics right now, Bill. But I promise, we're working on it."

"Good. Because we're going to stay on this story. And in the meantime, you're a stand-up guy for coming in."

* * *

O'Reilly and I don't disagree about the downside of the Internet. But I use it far more than he does—that is, every hour of the day—so my perspective is slightly different.

On the one hand, as a writer, I find it great to be able to search through the *Boston Globe* archives and find the article from 1992 in which Barney Frank begins promoting the subprime mortgages that eventually led to the financial meltdown.

On the other hand, I got burnt early on when an irrationally exuberant James Bond fan decided that my writing was the problem with the Bond films. He posted this on a Bond fan website, and some two hundred replies later—aided, abetted, and egged on by similarly irrationally invested Bond fans—the trolls came to the conclusion that the only way to "fix" the movies was to kill me, and they posted my home phone number and address to make that happen.

To quote the musician Sting, "I never saw no miracle of science / that didn't go from a blessing to a curse."

You can't imagine the stress this caused in my family, or the number of security measures we were told to put in place by law enforcement authorities, and that we still practice to this day.

And I'm a very small fish. Even I can't imagine what O'Reilly goes through on a daily basis. He hardly ever talks about it.

Let me be clear here: I'm not looking for sympathy. These things come with the territory. The same way it seems that no matter what piece of satire or parody I publish these days, someone blows it up to the size of a Macy's Thanksgiving Day Parade float filled with self-righteous indignation and tweets out to their 167 followers that I *must* be fired.

What really concerns me—and should concern you—are the issues of privacy and the way we're all getting gamed by the Internet.

Have you heard those ads on the radio for "reputation management," from companies that promise they can bury negative information about you, or your business, that might pop up in Internet search results? Last night, a friend e-mailed asking if I could point him to a news story that explained Hillary Clinton's e-mail problems.

So, I did a Google search. And although I should have known better, the results were surprising even to me: the first one hundred links that came up were either about how Secretary Clinton had told the truth, how it was all a Republican plot, or that it was a "nothing burger."

It wasn't until the third or fourth search page that I found anything that even resembled an objective analysis.

What's the explanation for this?

Just like those ads on the radio for reputation management, somebody manipulated those search results. It might have been Google itself, or an outside company hired by the Clinton campaign. I have no proof of who did it either way, but what I *do* know is that despite the claims that search results are "computer generated" by a "nonpartisan algorithm," the truth is that somebody, somewhere, a live human being, worked to give more "weight" and "authority" to the *Huffington Post* opinion pieces than to other websites. Thus, the negative stories about the e-mails were buried, deep in the search results.

During the 2016 presidential campaign, Facebook admitted to downplaying conservative websites, and promised to fix the bias. And Twitter has often been accused of banning conservative voices and ignoring trending topics that don't conform to its CEO's politics.*

---

* During the 2016 presidential campaign, Silicon Valley's financial support was estimated to run as high as 9:1 for Clinton over Trump. The tech titans who backed Clinton included Facebook's CEO, Mark Zuckerberg; Facebook's chief operating officer, Sheryl Sandberg (who allegedly shared Facebook's data with Clinton's advisers); Eric Schmidt, executive chairman of Google's parent company, Alphabet (which bankrolled a start-up called The Groundwork, which was hired by the Clinton campaign to promote voter turnout); plus Apple's Tim Cook and LinkedIn's Reid Hoffman.

Meanwhile, almost all the websites you visit have the ability to track you—and can figure out your age, your race, your gender, your sexual orientation, where you live, how much money you make, who your friends are, whether you're single or married, how many kids you have, what your hobbies are, what sports teams you follow, what ails you medically, and how you lean politically. And they tailor their news accordingly, serving up stories that keep you clicking on their web pages, and to some extent, ignoring the news that will drive you away.

This isn't good for people on the right or the left. It only adds to the sense of division, and the feeling that we're now living in two different countries.

So, other than watch O'Reilly (Hey! He'd stop talking to me if I didn't get that plug in), what's the Old School solution here?

Be skeptical. Read outside your comfort zone. And recognize that we are now living in an online version of *The Wizard* of Oz—where there really is a computer Wizard behind that curtain, manipulating all of us.

An Internet Glossary for Old Schoolers

Ever have the feeling that Internet-savvy people, sometimes called "The Digerati," are speaking a different language?

Well . . . you're right.

And while cyberspace is not all that compatible with Old School wisdom, it is always helpful to know what the other side is doing.

This glossary may help you do that.

Metrics. Internet-speak for statistics (how many people visit a website, how long they stay, etc.), but considering that up to 50 percent of all website visits are made by nonhuman "bots," robotic programs searching to index websites, hack them, or copy information—perhaps we should be now saying, "There are three kinds of lies: lies, damned lies, and Internet metrics."*

Cookies. Tiny digital files that explain why, after you've searched for "Bermuda Hotels" on one website, ads for Bermuda Hotels start showing up on every website you visit. Hopefully, this will clear things up for O'Reilly, who still thinks "cookies" refers to Fig Newtons.

Hot takes. Fast, off-the-cuff "instant analysis" pieces posted on websites in response to breaking news. All too often these represent the exact opposite of what we were all taught in school, which was to *think* before we write.

---

* Source: the Internet security firm Imperva Incapsula's annual Bot Traffic Report.

Search engine optimization. Imagine if O'Reilly had stayed in the house painting business. (Somewhere, a politician is reading this, saying, "I only wish . . .") He may be a Luddite, but he has a website. And above all else, he wants to remain "The #1 house painter on Long Island for 41 years and counting." So, what does he do? He hires a search engine optimization company to tweak his site, so whenever anyone searches for "best painter on Long Island," the O'Reilly Old School Paint and Plaster Company appears first in the search results. Then, the search engine optimization guys perform a similar trick with all the positive reviews O'Reilly's company's work has received across the Net—so the first two hundred search results are all about how great O'Reilly is, and the *one* negative review from a Snowflake ("Great painter, but his men don't recycle their water bottles!") shows up on the fourth page of the search results, where no one will ever find it.

Apple. The tech company with a social conscience—except, some say, when it comes to paying taxes,* maintaining decent working conditions in its Chinese factories, and helping the FBI catch terrorists.

Click bait. Trivial, inaccurate, or time-wasting website content hyped with sensational headlines where the main purpose is to get you to "click through" to additional Web pages (e.g., "19 Ways the O'Reilly Factor Is More Interesting than Cat Videos,"

---

* According to Marketwatch.com, "The European Commission has demanded that Ireland recoup roughly €13 billion ($14.5 billion) in what it claims are unpaid taxes from Apple . . . Apple has the most [untaxed] cash outside the U.S. of any U.S. company, at more than $200 billion."

and "63 Times O'Reilly Asked Charles Krauthammer, 'Tell Me Where I'm Going Wrong Here'").

Emojis and Emoticons. The little symbols in e-mail or text messages meant to convey wit, irony, sagacity, shrewdness, apoplexy, chagrin, or despair—often used by people who don't know the meaning of the words *convey, wit, irony, sagacity, shrewdness, apoplexy, chagrin,* or *despair.* Put another way: After forty thousand years of civilization, we're back to cave paintings.

BFF, BAE. Internet initials of endearment meaning, respectively, "best friend forever" and "before anyone else." Think O'Reilly and Geraldo. On second thought, don't *ever* do that.

Going viral. The Internet age equivalent of being the Pet Rock. When something gets shared millions of times—as with the video of the woman laughing while wearing the Star Wars Chewbacca mask. Viral hits are everywhere for about three weeks, and then gone.

Memes (pronounced "meems"). Ideas that spread from the Internet. If you can bear to recall the 2016 presidential campaign, here's the difference: The video of Donald Trump and Billy Bush on that bus went viral. What followed—the commentary and the late-night jokes about Trump—were memes. Videos or posts go viral; ideas become memes.

Instagram. A subsidiary of Facebook with which people share pictures and videos. Sort of like the *USA Today* of social media: lots of visuals and bright colors, not too many words or thoughts.

Snapchat. An encrypted private messaging system, used mainly by millennials, to send short videos, pictures, and texts that are automatically deleted, and supposedly can never be recovered, after twenty-four hours. A Snapchat account would have been the perfect wedding present for Huma Abedin and Anthony Weiner.

The Sharing Economy. A misnomer. If money changes hands, you're not "sharing" a ride on Uber or "sharing" an apartment on Airbnb.

Twitter. A social media website for posting remarks that are limited to 140 characters. O'Reilly and Feirstein both know a semifamous TV news reporter (who is not an anchor and not on Fox News) who has sent out close to 91,000 tweets since 2010. This breaks down to 13,000 tweets a year, or 35 tweets a day—meaning more than one tweet *an hour, every hour, every day of the year*. Is this the definition of insane or what?*

Tweet storm. A barrage of angry tweets, often but not always with dubious results. (See Donald J. Trump, 2016 Electoral College results: For all the people who said, "A man who can't be trusted to handle his Twitter account can't be trusted with the nuclear codes," there was clearly a significant number of people who felt otherwise, and appreciated the way Trump fires back at his critics.)

---

* While this addresses one criticism of Twitter (that it seems like a fire hose of triviality), the larger issue concerns abuse and harassment. At a recent tech conference in Silicon Valley, this was cited as the reason that some celebrities and high-profile tech users have abandoned the service and, in terms of the general public, that Twitter's growth has stalled.

Trending on Twitter. We're not big fans of news stories that report on what's "blowing up" or "trending" on Twitter. Why? Because they only represent what *people who use Twitter* are saying. It's cheap journalism, and far too easy, to take the unhinged rantings of a handful of lunatics on Twitter and write up a story implying that it's indicative of what everyone is thinking, and use this to tar everyone on the left or the right as crazy, vile, or worse.*

Trolling. The act of commenting, in a negative and usually off-topic way, on something, just to start an argument. It's like throwing chum in the water to incite the sharks. For example, sooner or later any positive article about George W. Bush will have someone comment, "Bush lied, people died." Likewise, any positive article about Hillary Clinton will eventually see the comment "She should be in jail." The parlor game here is to see how long it takes before the commenters devolve into calling each other racist, sexist, fascist, or Hitler. Extra points for the first citation of "Faux News."

Concern trolling. A variation on regular trolling, this is when someone *pretends* to be concerned about an issue in order to post all sorts of negative things about it. For example, someone who believes ESPN has become too political, and resents that, might post, "I love ESPN, but I'm worried the politics are driving

---

* According to the company's quarterly reports, Twitter has been hovering around 310 million monthly users worldwide for several years. Only 20 percent of those users are located in America—meaning, only around 60 million Americans use the service at least once a month. While this appears to be a significant number, it's worth noting that Twitter does not break that number down into daily users, number of business accounts (every pizza joint in America begging, "Follow me!), or number of fake accounts you can buy as followers with a simple Google search for as little as $14 per 1,000 followers.

away viewers." This then opens the door for the commenter to list all the ways he believes ESPN has become too political. It's a neat trick that was used frequently by Hillary Clinton supporters during the 2016 presidential campaign to highlight the shortcomings of Bernie Sanders: "I love Bernie, but I'm worried he's too radical to win a general election." And thus, out spewed all the negative talking points about the senator.

Sock puppetry. When a journalist comments favorably on his own writing, but under a fake name. The source of the term goes back to the 1950s, when the puppeteer Shari Lewis introduced Lamb Chop, a sassy, back-talking lamb that was little more than a sock with sewn-on eyes and fleece.

Virtue signaling. Using social media to preen and show what a good person you are by tweeting out empty sentiments such as "If Trump gets elected, I'm moving to Canada," or, after a disaster or tragedy, "My thoughts and prayers go out to the families." The best example of this may well be "I stand with Charlie Hebdo." Really? How, exactly, do you 'stand' with the French cartoonists who were murdered by Islamic terrorists, other than by signaling your virtue by posting, "I stand with Charlie Hebdo"? Are you actually willing to do something about it, other than send out a tweet? Probably not.

Fake news. When the mainstream media reported that Trump's campaign was falling apart, Obamacare was saving people money, and Hillary Clinton had a 99 percent chance of winning, it was "real" news. When an Internet website says otherwise, the mainstream media say it's fake. Go figure.

Facebook. The eight-hundred-pound gorilla of social messaging applications. Nothing matches its reach, influence, or ability to pry into your life. As professional skeptics, we'll admit to being slightly suspicious of Facebook's user numbers. Few of our friends use it. Most of our high school buddies' accounts haven't been updated in years. We know of too many people with multiple accounts (brand managers, political operatives, and businesspeople) with which they anonymously track their competitors.

According to a 2016 Facebook's quarterly report, almost 160 million Americans (nearly half the country) spend close to fifty minutes a day on Facebook. Why? If *you* know, please let us know. If you can break your family and friends away from their machines for a few minutes to explain it, the conversation might be as helpful to you, and your relationships, as it is to us.

Until then, remember that sooner or later all technology passes. Phonograph records and DVDs gave way to streaming. IBM gave way to Microsoft. AOL and Yahoo were surpassed by Google and Facebook.

It's entirely possible that one day you will look at all your Facebook "friends" (the former business associates, fleeting acquaintances, and ancient classmates) and wonder if Facebook's epitaph will ultimately be "There was a reason you fell out of touch with all those people in the first place."

Facebook may be a passing fad.

But Old School—that's forever.

11

Old School Politics

Sometimes people are neither Old Schoolers nor Snowflakes. Both Hillary Clinton and Donald Trump fall into this category, which we will explain later. For now, though, O'Reilly will take a look at a big Snowflake who became president.

Martin Van Buren.

I know, I know, you were just discussing him last night. How could you not? The guy dripped with charisma—the JFK of his day.

Well, not exactly.

Marty was the eighth president and the first one actually born an American citizen. Raised in upstate New York, he became involved in politics at age seventeen and never left it.

That is *not* a good sign.

Old Marty should have at least milked a few cows or something.

Anyway, Van Buren worked his way up by cutting all kinds of sleazy deals. Ethics weren't exactly bogging him down.

He became known as the "Little Magician" because he could get things done in the back room all the while looking exactly like the mayor of Munchkinland who told Dorothy to skip down the yellow brick road.

After razzle-dazzling them in New York, MVB went to Washington as a senator. Realizing that he needed a patron, the diminutive Marty eventually grabbed onto the coattails of Andrew Jackson, an Old School guy if there ever was one. Jackson was a force of nature, and if you messed with him, bad things could happen fast.

Van Buren, a complete milquetoast, became Jackson's "fixer," his go-to guy when questionable deals had to be made. His reward? He became Jackson's second-term running mate in 1832, and was

The original Snowflake

handed the presidential nomination in 1936, a race Van Buren won by defeating four Whig opponents, two of whom Charlie Sheen could have beaten.

Now for a story that will make this entire book worthwhile.

Lacking any kind of principled direction, Martin Van Buren was a Snowflake, no doubt. But he is directly responsible for what could be the most used word on the planet.

That word is *okay*.

That's right, many wordsmiths believe that affirmation is said more times by human beings than any other utterance.

Here's how it came into being.

Van Buren was born in the small town of Kinderhook, outside Albany, New York. As he became more influential with Andrew Jackson, political folks began to notice how obsequious Marty was. He usually called Jackson "General," which the crusty Battle of New Orleans veteran liked.

Marty's behavior toward Jackson was very similar to Ed McMahon's relationship with Johnny Carson, one that lasted three decades on late-night TV.

"You are correct, sir," McMahon would bellow to Carson, pretty much backing up everything the *Tonight Show* star said on air. After most every joke, Carson received a booming laugh from the affable McMahon, who then would often yell, "Hey-oh."

Somewhere, Martin Van Buren was smiling.

As he rose in power thanks to Jackson, Marty was nicknamed Old Kinderhook by the pols and pundits in Washington, which was then shortened to OK.

After a while, as the story goes, because Van Buren agreed with everything Jackson said or did, *OK* morphed into the ultimate verbal agreement as it spread across the land and eventually around the world.

All thanks to a kiss-butt Snowflake.

Marty eventually got his. In his first year as president, the U.S. economy collapsed, and it never really recovered while he was in the White House. Unfortunately, Van Buren didn't have George W. Bush as his predecessor, so he couldn't blame the disaster on him. Thus, Marty got pounded.

Van Buren quickly became known as "Martin Van Ruin" and was trounced by William Henry Harrison in the election of 1840. Harrison was another Old School guy who might have shot Van Buren if he had given him any jazz.

Known as "Tippecanoe" for defeating the brother of Native American chief Tecumseh in battle, President Harrison died just thirty-two days after being inaugurated, from a respiratory situation.

Vice President John Tyler, a Snowflake who fathered fifteen children with two wives, took over.

Throughout our history, we've had both Old School leaders and Snowflakes in charge of the country. The litmus test for an Old School politician is simple: prioritize looking out for the folks over yourself, and stand for something noble.

Abraham Lincoln and George Washington set the gold standard for Old School politicians. Teddy and Franklin Roosevelt also get that designation, as do John Adams, James Madison, Harry Truman, Ronald Reagan, and both Bushes.

Thomas Jefferson and John Kennedy are tough calls. They were definitely not Snowflakes, but Old School? Debatable.

Jefferson was brilliant at writing the Declaration of Independence, but he essentially sat out the Revolutionary War. He wanted no part of a military commission he could easily have secured. So, he watched the war play out from his plantation in western Virginia, all the while keeping an eye on his slaves. Perhaps too close an eye, as there is evidence of physical interactions with Sally Hemings. That has not been proven 100 percent, but few would be surprised if it were. Exploiting slaves is definitely not Old School behavior.

JFK also used his position as president to develop an active "social life," which was not looking out for the folks, to say the least. Old School people are sinners like every human, but unselfish patterns of behavior are necessary to get the OS designation.

That brings us to President Barack Obama, another tough call on the Old School front. He was the most liberal president in American history, but that does not automatically eliminate him from Old School status. Liberal thinkers such as Pope Francis and the late Tip O'Neill are definitely Old School guys. It's all about putting a sincerely held philosophy into action and trying to do good things.

While in the White House, Barack Obama set a powerful example as a family man. In this age of disloyalty, he demonstrated to the world that a stable, loving family was a super positive achievement. That is Old School to the max.

Yet, Mr. Obama's ardent leftist view of the world kept him from truly looking out for the folks on far too many occasions. Here is a very specific example of that.

Millions of American children, many of them minorities, are trapped in a cycle of poverty and violence. We all know the stats: more than 70 percent of African American babies are now born out of wedlock. Without a stable family, kids are at a major disadvantage in our hypercompetitive society.

So, President Obama came up with a terrific initiative to help minority children in the inner city. It's called My Brother's Keeper. Basically, it works like this: Private companies provide mentors to kids all over the country. The one-on-one interaction allows caring, successful adults to give scholastic and social guidance to young people—kind of like the Big Brother and Big Sister programs. I endorsed My Brother's Keeper on the air because it is a good thing for America.

A short time later, I received an invitation to the White House, where Mr. Obama was introducing twenty young men from Chicago who were participating in MBK. I showed up and was immediately dismayed to see Al Sharpton in attendance. This sent negative signals to me right off the bat because Sharpton is an opportunistic charlatan.

Quick story to back that up. A few years ago, Sharpton told me that his charitable foundation was low on funds and could not provide his annual free holiday dinners to the poor in Harlem. So, I gave the charity twenty-five thousand dollars with a request that the donation be kept private. I don't do things like that for publicity.

The holiday dinners were served.

Shortly after that, Sharpton went on his TV show and implied that I was a racist over some analysis I had put forth on *The O'Reilly Factor.*

He's quite a guy.

Anyway, after the White House My Brother's Keeper event ended, President Obama walked over to thank me for supporting the initiative. It was a kind gesture, and I told him that I would soon be sending him an idea that would help the program get some positive publicity.

Without violating confidences, I was well on the way to setting up a huge rock concert complete with corporate sponsorship and a national TV airing. The money raised, tens of millions of dollars, would all go to My Brother's Keeper, and the concert would garner massive publicity for the noble effort.

Sensitive to any political stuff, I told the White House that I did not want any mention of my involvement. I'd get the venue and the talent gratis, and they could handle the rest.

The event never happened.

I don't know why.

Everything was set to go.

I strongly suspect that politics is the reason the show did not go on. President Obama could have made the concert a reality simply by snapping his fingers.

By the way, when was the last time you heard anything about My Brother's Keeper?

So, I cannot bestow Old School status on Barack Obama. But I don't think he's a Snowflake, as he lives his life consistently under a defined value system. He's just one of legions of folks who let ideology and opportunism prevent them from being truly effective— something Old School adherents don't do.

Finally, in order for America to avoid drowning under the politically correct contagion and the weak-kneed social policies that Snowflakes die for (not literally—that crew wouldn't die for anything), a very strong Old School leader will have to emerge from the chaos currently gripping the United States.

But take heart. The country could not have been any worse off than it was under President James Buchanan.

Then Abraham Lincoln arrived.

Over to you, Feirstein.

* * *

To quote the actor Jim Carrey, channeling Martin Van Buren: Well, *okay*, Bill.

While I agree that it's important to recognize that Thomas Jefferson owned slaves and very possibly fathered six children with Sally Hemings—particularly given his opposition to slavery and his fights to end the slave trade—I'm going to take issue with you on JFK and President Obama.

For me, above all else, JFK was the quintessential Old School Cold Warrior. Even before the Cuban Missile Crisis, the race to beat the USSR to the moon, and his dispatching four hundred Green Berets to Vietnam to help prevent the spread of communism in Southeast Asia, he summed up his philosophy best in his inaugural address:

"Let every nation know, whether it wishes us well or ill, that we shall pay any price, bear any burden, meet any hardship, support any friend, oppose any foe to assure the survival and the success of liberty."

Then there's Barack Obama. Sorry, but if we defined an Old School person in the opening chapter of this book as someone who says what he's going to do and then does it, then, for me, Obama was Old School all the way.

He did exactly what he said he was going to do—and used every lever he had to accomplish his progressive agenda—even sitting down with O'Reilly for three interviews.

I'm not talking about outcomes here. Nor am I addressing a friend in the GOP who defines a community organizer as "Somebody who riles up the neighborhood, calls a press conference, and leaves everybody else to clean up the mess."

Rather, I'm going back to the old saw "Elections have consequences." Barack Obama got elected not once, but twice. And, if we're going to be honest, had he been a Republican, the GOP might be cheering his accomplishments. I know O'Reilly dissents. But I think Barack Obama stayed true to himself, even though not all his policies worked out that well.

And let's not forget one other thing: When Obama ran for president, we were no longer the country that was altogether willing to bear any burden or pay any price to police the world anymore.

I realize steam may be coming out of the ears of people reading this book. Bear with me for a moment. We'll get to the consequences and the outcomes of the Obama years soon enough.

Just to put all this into perspective, as the Obama years recede in the rearview mirror, let's go back to the presidency of George H. W. Bush. He was an Old School guy all the way, with quiet dignity and great faith in America, from his time as a naval aviator during World War II to the decades he spent in public service. And perhaps nothing exemplifies this better, and shows the way for all of us, than the letter he left in the Oval Office for Bill Clinton after his stinging defeat to Clinton in the 1992 presidential election. It goes right back to Lincoln and his famous first inaugural address:

"We are not enemies, but friends. We must not be enemies. Though passion may have strained it must not break our bonds of affection. The mystic chords of memory, stretching from every battlefield and patriot grave to every living heart and hearthstone all over this broad land, will yet swell the chorus of the Union, when again touched, as surely they will be, by the better angels of our nature."

Here is the letter George H. W. Bush left Bill Clinton:

Jan. 20, 1993

Dear Bill,

When I walked into this office just now I felt the same sense of wonder and respect that I felt four years ago. I know you will feel that, too.

I wish you great happiness here. I never felt the loneliness some Presidents have described.

There will be very tough times, made even more difficult by criticism you may not think is fair. I'm not a very good one to give advice; but just don't let the critics discourage you or push you off course.

You will be *our* President when you read this note. I wish you well. I wish your family well.

Your success now is our country's success. I am rooting hard for you.

Good Luck—George

* * *

Now, let's talk outcomes.

Every year, Chapman University conducts a survey across the nation to find out what Americans fear most.

Do you want to guess what the top answer was in 2016?

It wasn't terrorism.

It wasn't another financial meltdown.

It wasn't climate change, losing a loved one, going broke, or getting involved in another war.

The number one fear for Americans in 2016, by a margin of almost 20 percent, was corrupt government officials.

Let's say that again: When the survey was taken in April 2016, more people feared government corruption than a terrorist attack, a life-threatening illness, or being the victim of a violent crime.

And that was *before* Bill Clinton met with Attorney General Loretta Lynch on the tarmac in Phoenix . . .

. . . *before* James Comey said that despite her being "extremely careless" with classified information, "no reasonable prosecutor" would bring a case against Hillary Clinton . . .

. . . and *before* we learned from the WikiLeaks e-mails about the rush to wipe the email server after a subpoena had been issued, news reporters advising the DNC on how to attack Trump, Donna Brazile passing along the moderator's questions before the debates, the dinners John Podesta shared with a high-ranking official in the Justice Department who was investigating the e-mail scandal, the plotting against Bernie Sanders's campaign, and the apparent collusion between the Clinton Foundation and the State Department in what seemed to be pay-to-play influence pedaling scheme.

And all *that* was before James Comey reopened the investigation into the e-mail server because of something the FBI found on the computers and cell phones Anthony Weiner had used to send lewd pictures to a fifteen-year-old girl . . .

. . . and *then* reversed himself three days before the election.

You couldn't make this up if you tried.

And you couldn't find a more insidious way to undermine Americans' faith and trust in our government.

By Election Day 2016, we'd become a nation where large parts of the country no longer trusted Washington or the media.

We'd become a nation where large parts of the country had grown tired and suspicious of the Friday afternoon document dumps, where the hope seemed to be that the latest unseemly news would get buried by sports stories over the weekend.

Large parts of the country had grown tired of sending politicians to Washington, where they didn't do what they'd promised, and yet somehow *miraculously* made millions in office—before exiting through a gold-plated revolving door to Wall Street, Silicon Valley, or a K Street lobbying shop.

Large parts of the country had grown tired of celebrities hectoring them about climate change and gun control, while flying around in private jets and making movies filled with gunplay, and then screaming about their First Amendment rights when the audience pushed back and said they were not going to buy their records or movies.

Large parts of the nation had grown tired of the talking points, the too-cute-by-half parsing of language ("I didn't set a red line [on Syria]. The world set a red line"), and politicians who seemed to think that most of the country was populated by idiots who couldn't handle the truth or spot a lie.

People had grown tired of polls that had been endlessly tweaked and massaged, not to reflect what they were thinking, but to influence the outcome of elections.

They'd become tired of politicians who focus-tested every idea and every issue, not to find out what concerned us, but to determine what the politician should run on and where he should stand on an issue.

They were fed up with the words *optics, messaging, flyover, Dumpster fire,* and *narrative.*

We'd become a nation where half the country believed that the FBI, the Justice Department, the IRS, and most of the media had become toxically politicized—while the other half of the country either didn't believe this, didn't know about it, or didn't want to hear about it—until it was somebody on *their* side getting gored.

This last point is nothing new. As Mark Twain is said to have observed over a hundred years ago, "If you don't read the newspaper, you're uninformed. If you read the newspaper, you're misinformed."

And this points us to what may have been the saddest headline of the 2016 presidential race. Remember the Pentagon Papers, the secret documents leaked by military analyst Daniel Ellsberg revealing what Lyndon Johnson had said about the scope of our involvement in the Vietnam War? And do you remember the way the *New York Times* fought all the way to the Supreme Court to publish the Pentagon Papers, and eventually won a Pulitzer Prize for it?

Consider this headline from the *Times* regarding WikiLeaks, from the October 18, 2016, edition, just two weeks after the paper published leaked copies of Donald Trump's tax returns:

"Just Because It's Hacked, Doesn't Mean It's Important."*

What's the Old School response to this?

You're Old School if you can remember when you could read a story about politics without wondering, What's the reporter's agenda? What is she leaving out? How is she trying to spin me, what ax do the anonymous sources have to grind, and what's the real truth here?

* * *

At the beginning of this chapter, O'Reilly wrote about the way Snowflake Martin Van Buren was followed, years later, by Abraham Lincoln.

In the aftermath of the insane 2016 presidential campaign—and all that's followed—we're definitely living in divided, unsettled times.

But take heart: the republic will survive.

One way or another, as Lincoln so hoped in his first inaugural address, America will be touched again by the better angels of our nature.

---

* To be fair, the *Times'*s article on WikiLeaks does acknowledge the paper's role in publishing both the purloined Pentagon Papers and the Trump tax returns. But the reporter tips his hand, revealing what he really thinks about WikiLeaks, in the last paragraph, where he writes, "Where there's a smoking gun, there isn't always fire."

12

Are You a Snowflake?

If there's one real indicator of Old School behavior, it's that we have a solid philosophy that emphasizes generosity and loyalty.

Is someone close to you in danger of slipping and sliding in the realm of blizzards and mush?

If so, this field guide to identifying flaky behavior may be of some help.

* * *

You might be a Snowflake if you're twenty-seven and still living in your parents' basement.

You're almost certainly a Snowflake if you're thirty-seven and still living with roommates.

And you're definitely a Snowflake if you blame either of these living situations on the government and believe it's the government's responsibility to take care of your every need.

You're a Snowflake if you believe no one has a right to privacy.

You're a Snowflake if you can't understand why an employer might not want to hire you because of what you've tweeted or posted on Facebook.

You're a Snowflake if you think it might be "fun" to go rock climbing in the Kurdistan region of Iraq (as three U.S. citizens did in 2009) and wind up in an Iranian prison . . . and you somehow think the Iranians are going to go easy on you because you describe yourself as a "social justice warrior" who doesn't agree with U.S. foreign policy.

You're a Snowflake if you think the rest of the world is just like us.

You're a Snowflake if you're among the 25 percent of millennials who, in a YouGov.com survey in 2016, thought George W. Bush killed more people than Josef Stalin.

You're a Snowflake if you think that aside from the political prisoners, the human rights violations, and the lack of free speech, Fidel Castro was actually a pretty good guy.

And as long as we're talking about Cuba, you're definitely a Snowflake if you're wearing a Che Guevara T-shirt and don't realize that Che would have had no compunction in killing you for about half the things you believe in—and "liberating" your T-shirt right off your back.

Chances are you're a Snowflake if you went to a university whose marketing brochure contains more about diversity than it does about math, science, or engineering.

You're a Snowflake if you agree with the linguistics professor at the University of California–Berkeley who wrote in *Time*

If Che Guevara could see you wearing this T-shirt, he would not be amused.

magazine that the investigation into Hillary Clinton's e-mail server was all about sexism and not national security.

You're a Snowflake if you needed Play-Doh and crayons to deal with the results of the 2016 presidential election.

You're a Snowflake if you blamed "internalized misogyny" for Hillary's loss.

You're a Snowflake if you agreed with Hampshire College's decision to ban the American flag from campus after Donald Trump's victory because it triggered fear among the Snowflakes who go there.

You're a Snowflake if instead of being concerned about posting your good grades in college, you were far more interested in posting your list of grievances.

You're a Snowflake if the first thing that comes to mind when

you hear the word *deconstructivism* isn't a sledgehammer, a work crew, or a trip to Home Depot.

You're a Snowflake if you know what the word *semiotics* means. We don't.

You're a Snowflake if you actually believed any presidential candidate who promised that college education would be free.

You're a Snowflake if you graduated with a degree that contains the words *comparative, ethnic*, or *studies*.

You're a Snowflake if you can't understand why that degree did not prepare you for *any job at all*...

... other than teaching the next generation of Snowflakes, at yet another university, about how to get another degree that contains the words *comparative, ethnic*, or *studies*.

You're a Snowflake if you use the word *mansplaining*.

You're a Snowflake if your primary source of political news is comedians on late-night TV.

You're a Snowflake if you look to celebrities for advice about how to cast your vote.

You're a Snowflake if you hate Fox News, particularly O'Reilly, but have never actually watched the channel.

And you're all but living in a snowdrift—no, make that a *blizzard*—if you tune in to watch *The View* every single day of the week, hoping Barbara Walters will return.

You're a Snowflake if you think there's an app that's going to solve all your problems.

You're a Snowflake if you believe that a mass-produced piece of consumer electronics—like, say, an Apple watch—makes you a special person.

You're a Snowflake if you think all corporations are evil—except for the Silicon Valley start-up you work for, where you're

hoping to make millions when it floats an initial public offering on the stock market—which is evil, too.

And you must have been buried by an avalanche or living in an igloo if you swoon for the politics of Elizabeth Warren, and seriously believed that a Hillary Clinton presidency would do *anything* to rein in the banks, solve the problem of inequality, or tax the rich.

You're a Snowflake if you don't understand why people shop at Costco, but have never been in one of the stores.

You're a Snowflake if you refer to people who have kids as "breeders."

You're a Snowflake if you feel marginalized by your college mascot.

You're a Snowflake if you can actually tell all the superhero movies apart.

You're a Snowflake if you think that unless Mexican food is cooked by Mexicans, Italian food by Italians, and Chinese food by Chinese, it's not just cultural appropriation, but a crime against humanity.

And you're definitely a Snowflake if you think the legalization of recreational marijuana won't have terrible repercussions—unless you're currently too stoned to see the negative impact it's already having in states like Colorado.

You're a Snowflake if you believe that people in the military or law enforcement aren't as smart or as enlightened as you are.

You're a Snowflake if your idea of protest involves burning down the neighborhood where you live.

You're a Snowflake if you think looting a 7-Eleven is going to advance your cause.

You're a Snowflake if you don't see something odd about two thousand people flying from all over the world to attend a climate

change conference in Switzerland when they could just as easily have "saved the planet" by using Skype or e-mail.

You're a Snowflake if you think climate change is responsible for the rise of ISIS.

You're a Snowflake if you find any or all of the following things offensive: Christmas carols, the Easter bunny, Columbus Day, Pilgrims, beauty contests, NASCAR, Thanksgiving, pro football, cheerleaders, nativity scenes, "The Star-Spangled Banner," and the Pope.

You're a Snowflake if you believe that anyone who disagrees with you isn't just wrong, but despicable.

Or deplorable.

You're a Snowflake if you've cut off friends or members of your family because they don't mirror your every political view.

You're a Snowflake if you think it's amusing to let your teenaged kids drink alcohol or smoke pot.

You're a Snowflake if every single day, from the moment you get up in the morning, until the time you go to bed at night, every time you enter a store, turn on the TV, drive a car, or go on the Internet, you find something you get outraged about.

And it's all *unforgivable.*

You're a Snowflake if you can't accept the joy, or the happiness, that others find in the pastimes, hobbies, or the religious beliefs that you find ridiculous.

You're a Snowflake if you're constantly telling others not to be "so judgmental," but you can't see how judgmental *you are* about everything and everyone, all the time.

Finally, you're not just a Snowflake, but someone who is in for a long, dark, cold winter's night if you can't accept the quirks, the flaws, and the foibles that separate us from Snowflakes—and make us such perfectly imperfect human beings, one and all.

13

Are You Old School?

Are you entitled to wear the Old School varsity jacket?

Obviously that's a trick question.

Only Snowflakes feel as if they're entitled to everything.

For Old School folks, everything you accomplish and everything you do is earned—especially that jacket.

But if you're still unsure of your OS status, the following may offer some guidance.

* * *

You're Old School if you know how to drive a stick.

You're Old School if you can remember when you could look under the hood of a car and still have some idea how to fix it.

You're Old School if you can remember when you could read a sports column without getting a political opinion.

You're Old School if you miss the days when ordering a cup of coffee didn't include the words *Venti, Grande, latte,* or *soya.*

You're Old School if you can remember when a twenty-dollar bill seemed like a lot of money.

You're Old School if you don't believe in "best guess" spelling. Yo, it's *night,* not *nite!*

You're Old School if you can't believe that *manipulatives* is the new word for building blocks, and "gross motor room" is the new name for a gym.

You're Old School if you can remember when it actually seemed like fun to go to an airport.

You're Old School if you can remember when people got dressed up to fly on a plane.

You're Old School if you *don't* recline the airline seat all the way back.

You're Old School if you're amazed at all the incredible things you can do with your smartphone—except for actually conducting a conversation.

You're Old School if you can remember when the phrases "We're breaking up" and "I'm losing you" were about your love life, not your cell phone.

You're Old School if you can't understand why stores that you visit once a year insist on sending you an e-mail *every single day of the week.*

You're Old School if you feel that you now spend half your waking hours deleting all those unwanted e-mails.

You're Old School if you look at pictures of young women on a red carpet and your first thought is that they should go home and get dressed.

You're Old School if you look at the 219 kinds of toothpaste for

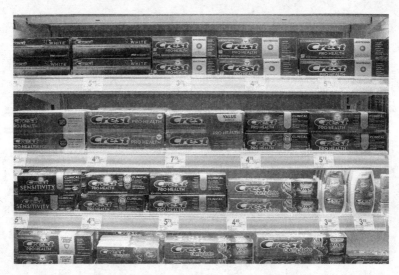

Seriously? Hundreds of kinds of toothpaste???

sale at CVS and end up buying the same brand you've always used because, well, it's *toothpaste*.

You're Old School if you want to cancel cable TV because you don't like the idea of paying for 265 TV channels you never watch, yet somehow you never get around to actually canceling it.

You're Old School if you wonder why almost every late-night TV talk show host has decided to alienate half of America with his politics, and take the chance of losing them forever as viewers, when all most people want is a fast laugh before they go to bed.

You're Old School if you don't have a clue what kale is.

Or quinoa.

Or "ethically raised beef." In the end, it's just going to end up as hamburger anyway, isn't it?

You're Old School if you give your children proper names and resist the urge to go trendy and name them after fruits, weather patterns, sitcom stars, rock-and-roll musicians, or compass navigation points. Someday they'll thank you for it.

You're Old School if you think your children should at least be able to eat solid food before they get their first iPad.

Likewise, you're Old School if you wish we could go back to the days when kids didn't call adults by their first names.

You're Old School if you don't do your kids' homework for them.

You're Old School if you succeed at teaching those kids the difference between "want" and "need."

You're Old School if you don't try to get out of jury duty.

You're Old School if you've come to the conclusion that early voting may not be such a good idea.

You're Old School if you can't understand why it's okay to require a photo ID to enter your office building but it's "the end of democracy as we know it" if you're asked to show an ID before walking into a voting booth.

You're Old School if you don't care if it's paper or plastic.

You're Old School if you actually have ten items or less.

You're Old School if you root for the underdog.

You're Old School if you stand up during the national anthem.

You're Old School if you meet someone who says he's a "citizen of the world" and then ask him, "So, what embassy are you going to run to when you get into trouble?"

You're Old School if you still bend over to pick up a penny.

You're Old School if you measure twice and cut once.

You're Old School if you agree with the old adage "Don't go around thinking the world owes you a living. It owes you nothing. It was here first."

You're Old School if you put everything away in the kitchen before you go to bed at night.

You're Old School if you get up before dawn every morning and go to work.

You're Old School if you make sure your kids get to school on time.

You're Old School if you don't expect a trophy.

You're Old School if you don't expect a standing ovation just for doing the right thing.

You're Old School if you remember that everyone you meet is fighting a hard battle.

You're Old School if you get kinder with age.

Old School Musings

No question O'Reilly is an Old School guy who walks the walk.

But what exactly comprises that stroll?

Well, here are some snapshots.

O'Reilly will start, then Feirstein will join us.

As far as my life is concerned, I believe I was given certain gifts by a creator.

Who also endowed me with weakness.

My choice: how I deal with both. Yours, too.

Moderation is a good Old School trait. Ice cream and pizza make that hard for me. But no pineapple on the pizza, ever.

I keep T-shirts for decades. They remind me of stuff that happened in the past, mostly good stuff. It's kind of like a classic rock radio station: the songs transport you back. As an Old School guy, I respect the past and try to learn from it.

Plus, I hate shopping.

Even on the dopey computer: whenever I order off that, the stuff is too small. I'm up to 2XL. I weigh 210 pounds. What does Shaq do?

Old School folks often compare tech to "back in the day" stuff.

I never enter an elevator before a woman or before all inside walk out.

When talking with a person, I look him directly in the eye.

I go to church. I do not wear short pants there. Nor do I carry in a water bottle like some folks. As Lucy once said, "Good grief, Charlie Brown!"

When annoyed, I squint like Clint Eastwood's Dirty Harry. Harry Callahan didn't like punks. That's Old School. Didn't like politically correct bosses, either. More OS attitude.

Clint Eastwood. How O'Reilly learned to squint.

I'm not a small talk kind of guy, but I'll ask people I meet where they're from because that interests me and it can lead to a productive chat.

I swear occasionally but feel stupid afterward. Rap makes me cringe. Who is helped by that vile stuff? The Four Tops were Old School.

I have never borrowed money.

Every month, I pay my bills on time.

I never waste money but always tip generously. If I forget, it bothers me.

I don't use endearments like "honey" or "cupcake."

I'll mock those who do, if I have the energy.

Always want a clean house.

And car.

And person.

No tattoos for me or Botox or tummy tucks or anything. Going out the way I came in.

Cheated on a test when I was thirteen. It bothered me. Never cheated again.

Stole some groceries once, when I was poor. Bothered me. Never stole anything again.

The nuns gave me that conscience thing.

When I was a kid, the New York Giants center fielder Willie Mays was my idol. I didn't understand what he, Jackie Robinson, or other black players were going through after breaking the color barrier. I did understand when stupid kids in my all-white Levittown neighborhood disparaged African Americans, and I did not brook it. That led to a few physical confrontations.

Willie Mays was Old School because he played hard, was nice to kids, and generally conducted himself impeccably.

An Old School original

Old School adherents treat all people with respect. Just like Willie did.

I believe evil acts will eventually be punished. Seen far too many of them in my life. Social media have mainstreamed horrible conduct. I do not engage people on the Net very much. Prefer to actually talk to human beings.

If I know someone has lied to enhance his circumstances, I will not deal with that person—at all.

I have lied to protect people from harm but not to hurt anyone.

Helped both my parents once I had the resources to do so. Never disrespected them. I was a hell-raising kid, and they did their best. It pains me to see kids with bad parents. Plenty of that in this age of narcissism.

I treat kids the same way I treat adults: talk to them straight, try to make them laugh if I can.

I also talk straight to my dogs. They understand they live in an Old School home. I believe they like it but realize their options are limited. Told them they will be Snowflakes if they run away.

Can't quite get the handle of the patience thing, and I am sure that makes me annoying.

Especially in restaurants.

Bored with folks who embrace victimhood.

And with those who automatically believe allegations against people.

And with those who play the race and gender cards.

Bored with people who want others to "empower" them. Empower yourself by being honest and working hard.

Can't stand the texting addiction.

Despise greed. Couldn't get through that *Wolf of Wall Street* movie. Wanted to punch Leo.

Like the Spenser private detective books by the late Robert Parker. Ultimate Old School guy because he had a simple philosophy that mirrors my own: do what you say you'll do.

Read all the Dave Robicheaux novels by James Lee Burke because Old School behavior is at the heart of those books.

Plus, Old School people admire skill, and Burke's writing is off-the-chart good.

Don't buy stuff unless I need it. Give away lots of money to those in trouble through no fault of their own.

I don't feel guilty about earning big money, but know I'm kind of fortunate in that area. So, Old School posture demands that I give back.

Don't want my tax money going to people who use the

government's generosity to buy drugs or booze. All means-tested welfare should be supervised. I don't work hard so you can get high. If you have a disease, go for a cure. I'll help you with that.

Never been intoxicated in my life. Not boasting, just reporting. Bad things often happen when substances take over.

Seen too much damage from that.

I try to be reasonable with all. Often fail because of Irish temperament. Blaming it on the Celts.

Don't like it when folks blame others for their own shortcomings. Wait. I just did that. Geez.

Could never figure out how to react when I'm betrayed. Anger accomplishes nothing. The more successful you become, the more betrayal you'll face.

It's Old School to accept that kind of brutal punishment without melting down because all human beings get it. But that doesn't mean you walk away. Old School people will fight hard to protect others and themselves.

Also, OS adherents will seek justice but not go the vigilante route.

I believe my country is noble, but I admit that blacks, Native Americans, and early Asian immigrants got hammered by injustice.

Believe we should all do what we can today to relieve that past blot on the nation's résumé.

Don't believe, however, that past sins condemn present situations. Been to eighty countries, and the United States is the best.

Although I could live in Ireland, Australia, or Switzerland.

Never in Cuba, Russia, or China.

I respect folks who are kind. I watched Michelle Obama on a few occasions treat strangers so well that I was floored.

Believe Mrs. Obama is Old School.

Hope she takes that the right way.

Harry Truman, Bush the Elder, George Patton, Winston Churchill, Andrew Young, and Mike Wallace—all Old School guys, just to name a few.

Jacqueline Kennedy was Old School while in the White House. Don't know about the Onassis business.

Sally Ride, Laura Bush, Barbara Walters, Oprah, Jane Pauley, Mother Teresa, and Margaret Thatcher—all Old School gals, to name just a few.

My cousin Dickie Melton, who fought bravely in Vietnam while upholding his family's tradition, is the ultimate Old School guy.

He makes me look like a Snowflake.

On-screen, Humphrey Bogart, Spencer Tracy, John Wayne, and Clint Eastwood are Old School, which is why they endure.

Also, Meryl Streep, Sally Field, and Judi Dench. They always give performances far beyond.

James Bond doesn't get more Old School, and Sean Connery was the best. He's an Old School guy in person, too.

Feirstein knows that firsthand.

So, over to him.

* * *

Hey, Bill, let's forget about Connery for a moment. I'll get to him soon enough.

I feel like we've entered the "back of the big book" segment here. The "No Snowflake Zone," a confessional booth where "Father O'Reilly" is doling out hell, damnation, and absolution from the other side of a computer screen.

"Smote that Snowflake."

"Grow a spine."

"Are you kidding me?"

"Go forth and whine no more."

"I'll give Him the last word."

Fortunately, as you may have noticed over the course of these pages, O'Reilly has a sense of humor about this stuff.

It's the one Old School virtue he left off his list: Be self-deprecating. Ultimately, we're all just pushing rocks up a hill. Be able to laugh at yourself, and your own idiosyncrasies.

As for me, there's a line from Tom Wolfe's 1998 novel, *A Man in Full*, that has always stayed with me: "The only real possession you'll ever have is your character."

It's something I've tried to keep in mind as I've careened my way through adulthood, trying to be a good person, trying to do the right thing.

I'd like to think I've succeeded more than I've failed.

But, then, I've spent the last sixteen years in Hollywood, where the bar on these kind of things is awfully low. More than once, I've heard somebody say, "Hell, I'd stab *myself* in the back if it would get me a hit picture."

Even now, as I write this, a few weeks after the presidential election, I'm dealing with one of these issues of character.

It seems that one of my teenaged twins' best friends is a Trump supporter. The kid moved to LA several years ago, from a red state, and the two kids bonded over music and sports, and quickly became part of the same crowd.

On the morning after the election, the Trump kid was ridiculed and shut out, banished. Shamed, even by my own child.

When I heard that, I was beyond upset. My wife and I explained to our teenager:

We don't act like that.

We don't hate people because of their politics.

And we expect you to apologize to that kid, and become friends again, even if nobody else does.

Twenty-four hours later, our teenager reported back that it had been done. I was proud, and secretly happy that I didn't have to take the next step, otherwise known as the nuclear option: no Wi-Fi . . . *forever.*

Still, there remained something about this that bothered me. Our kids aren't all that political. And they'd never heard anything inside our house that would have promoted that kind of behavior.

I suspect it came from a classmate whose father is a demi-celebrity, who I knew had an "active" Twitter feed. Sure enough, when I looked him up, I found what amounted to a sewer pipe of raging invective, where every other tweet was "F this" and "F that" and "We've got to F up all those racist Trump voters."

I was appalled. And I could only wonder: How does a parent expect to have any moral authority over his children if this is the character he shows to the world?

Character, an Old School word. Set yourself as an example. Whom do we look to for inspiration? Whom do we admire?

Here are a few names I'd add to O'Reilly's list of Old Schoolers:

Bill Bradley, the Rhodes Scholar, New York Knicks basketball Hall of Famer, and former senator from my home state of New Jersey, who showed what it really means to be an athlete and a scholar by serving his country honestly and acting with class on the court.

Bob Woodward, for reminding us what it means to be an Old School journalist: interviews, shoe leather, and facts rather than opinions, gossip, and conjecture.

Condoleezza Rice, who grew up playing piano in segregated Birmingham, Alabama, where one of her schoolmates was murdered in a racist church bombing. She overcame that trauma, earning a PhD from the University of Denver, serving as the provost at Stanford, and becoming U.S. secretary of state.

Ralph Lauren, the designer who started by selling ties out of a drawer in the Empire State Building, and went on define American style. Then, he used his good fortune to fund cancer research and to help pay for the restoration of Old Glory, the flag that inspired "The Star-Spangled Banner."

The actor Tom Hanks—not *just* for the movies he's made like *Saving Private Ryan* and *Apollo 13*, which showed us how "ordinary men" find the courage to confront extraordinary challenges, but also for the simple, dignified speech he gave to his colleagues in the aftermath of the 2016 presidential election, when his candidate didn't win:

> *We are going to be all right because we constantly get to tell the world who we are. We constantly get to define ourselves as American... We have the greatest country in the world because we are always moving towards a more perfect union. That journey never ceases, it never stops. Sometimes, to quote a Springsteen song, it's "one step forward, two steps back," but we still aggregately move forward... Because if we do not move forward, what is to be said of us?*

* * *

Finally, there's Sean Connery.

The first time I saw him was from the backseat of a black 1960 Chevy Bel Air, at a drive-in movie theater, in Livingston, New Jersey. I must have been ten or eleven at the time. My parents were up front. *Goldfinger* was on the screen.

I was awed by the way Connery moved through the film, so cool and calm and witty, prowling for the bad guys in his custom-made suits, like a well-tailored panther. And I understood instinctively that

he was "The man everyone wanted to be, and every woman wanted to be *with* . . ." even if I was too young to know *why* they wanted to be with him. Or what they wanted to *do* together.

Born in Scotland, he was the son of bus driver and housekeeper. He worked as a milkman before joining the Royal Navy. After that, he earned money as a bodybuilder and an artist's model. He also worked as a coffin polisher before getting his big break: being cast as James Bond.

As a kid, I was too young to be able to separate the actor from the character. And I couldn't have known the way Bond would loom over not just my life, but *all* our lives in the coming decades, just like the Beatles.

Originally, Ian Fleming didn't think Connery was the right actor for the role. But after seeing *Dr. No*, he went back to his still-unfinished novel, *Thunderball*, and rewrote the beginning, giving 007 Sean Connery's Scottish heritage.

Thirty years later, when I was working on the Bond franchise at Pinewood Studios, outside London, I'd see Connery occasionally, walking around the lot.

I'd heard that he was from the Old School of acting (show up, do your job, get paid), and that he didn't suffer fools or fanboys gladly. So, I didn't try to meet him.

But years later, after I'd moved from writing the Bond movies to the video games, I got my chance.

My family and I had been invited to a picnic thrown by a Hollywood mogul the day before the Oscars. The four us walked up the hill to the house. My wife held hands with our daughter; I did the same, with our son. They were both still toddlers.

At the top of the hill, I bent over to pick Thomas up. And when I rose up to throw him over my shoulder, there was Sean Connery. Face-to-face, a foot away, watching this.

An Old School gentleman to the core

It took a moment for it to sink in. Was it really him? But one look in those eyes, the dark brown pools that held secrets in so many movies, and one glance at the eyebrows, which seemed forever lifted with a hint of wry expectation, confirmed it. I spoke first, daring to point at him:

"You're Sean Connery. I'm Bruce Feirstein. You were in a few Bond movies. I wrote a few Bond movies. We need to talk."

He blinked, and reared his head back, as if weren't used to anyone addressing him like this. Then he smiled.

"Shure, shure," he said, in the Scottish burr I'd grown up imitating. He pointed off at some picnic tables in the distance. "Come over and talk when you're ready."

"I will," I said, then added, nodding to the kid perched on my shoulder, "By the way, this is my son," I said, introducing him by his first name.

"Nice to meet you," Connery replied, repeating the name with droll amusement in his voice. Then he turned back to me. "I'll see you in a few minutes," and walked off.

The next voice I heard belonged to my wife. "Are you out of your mind?" she asked. "Did you hear the way you talked to him?"

I shrugged. "What was he going to do, kill me? Somehow, I don't think he's carrying a gun."

Twenty minutes later, this time with my daughter, I walked over to the table where Connery was having lunch. I kneeled on the ground next to him, bouncing her on my knee. He smiled at her. Their eyes met, and she looked away.

The two of us began to talk about the inside baseball of the Bond franchise. He said that he'd received the script for an upcoming *From Russia with Love* video game, and that he looked forward to voicing it, because his grandchildren played video games.

"I hope you were well paid," he said with a sly look, adding, "Make sure you cash the check."

I knew our time was short. I wanted to tell him how much I appreciated his work. Not so much Bond, but *The Untouchables* and *The Man Who Would Be King*, which has always been one of my favorite movies. But I'd taken up enough of his time already.

"I've got to be honest with you," he said. "Since I stopped making the Bond movies, I haven't seen a lot of them. And I don't think I've seen all yours."

If he expected me to be surprised by this, he was wrong.

"I know what you mean," I replied. "It's kind of like an old girl-friend who's getting married. You're happy for her, but you don't need to be invited to the wedding."

He started to laugh.

"But I've got be honest with you, too," I continued, then paused. "In every one of the scripts I wrote, in every line of dialogue, the only voice I heard was yours."

Connery looked at my daughter. She looked away again.

"I think the young lady is flirting with me," he said, deflecting my compliment.

"Somehow, I don't think she's the first," I replied.

Connery turned and scrutinized me. A look and a nod passed between us: the son of a bus driver who'd polished coffins to earn money speaking with the barkeep's grandson, who, at that moment, was thinking about the mysteries of life, and the unforeseeable path from the backseat of a Chevy Bel Air to this lawn in Beverly Hills.

Connery put his hand on his heart. "It goes from me," he said, moving his hand to my shoulder, "to you ... to her." Sean Connery leaned forward, placing a kiss on my daughter's forehead.

It was a moment of amazing, Old School grace.

The Old School Election

Five days before Donald Trump was elected president, O'Reilly told the nation that Hillary Clinton could lose. In a moment, I'll explain further.

The vote to elect Donald Trump president was the most stunning event I've witnessed in my more than forty years in journalism. And I think a strong case can be made that the Old School philosophy helped Trump, who is not Old School himself but who leans more that way than his opponent Hillary Clinton.

President Trump does not fit the classic Old School profile because he has largely led a life of privilege and he made his living by wheeling and dealing. Nothing wrong with that unless your deals compromise Old School values. We don't have the data to make that determination about Trump, so his OS status is undetermined.

However, he's definitely not a Snowflake.

At one time, I thought Hillary Clinton had Old School possibilities. She's a hard worker, been through a lot but stayed loyal to her husband, and has the respect of a good number of old friends.

I remember Mrs. Clinton calling me after I defended her about a controversy over money. I said on the *Factor* that those Americans raised in the working class always carry a bit of financial insecurity around with them, even after achieving economic success. At the time, Hillary Clinton was under fire for underestimating her financial position.

We talked about her Midwest upbringing, and she agreed that my assessment about money applied to her. It was a nice conversation about the frugal childhood environment both she and I had experienced.

Then came the presidential campaign.

Hoping to capture support from the Bernie Sanders/Elizabeth Warren crew, Secretary Clinton, who knows better, veered sharply left. She didn't have to take that path; Trump was so controversial that he was constantly on the defensive. All Hillary had to do was mainstream her message.

She could not accomplish that.

Instead, she played gender and identity politics, demonizing Trump as a cross between Henry VIII and David Duke. Day after day, she pounded Trump with so many personal attacks that regular folks became numb to them. Then there were the heavy implications that if you didn't support Mrs. Clinton, you were deficient—perhaps even racist, misogynistic, or homophobic.

That hyped up anger and mobilized support for Trump.

To be fair, Trump used personal attacks, too, especially with the "crooked Hillary" business. But because the left-wing press gleefully joined the Clinton campaign's strategy of personal assault, the deck looked stacked against Trump, and many Americans took notice.

I don't really think the State Department e-mail thing was a deciding factor in many votes. It was too nebulous, and had no direct connection to anybody's life. Yes, the FBI investigation got a lot of notice, but, once again, the numb factor kicked in with the folks because the whole thing was so chaotic.

In my opinion, the Clinton Foundation situation was more damaging because it is clear the charity was used to benefit the Clintons politically and financially. That's awful, and Mrs. Clinton had no answer.

Trump did not exploit the Clinton Foundation issue perhaps because his own charitable concern was so poorly run. But the scale was far less. Comparing the Clinton Foundation to Trump's deal is like comparing lobster to fish sticks.

In the end, though, it was a combination of values and issues that defeated Mrs. Clinton.

Among the things that Clinton espoused during the campaign were open borders, amnesty for undocumented folks already in the country, no restraints on abortion until birth, no corporate tax relief, and a continuation of the Obama doctrine of income redistribution through subsidized health care and massive federal giveaways to the have-nots.

She also did not stand up for law enforcement, which generally does a great job, and she ignored working-class whites almost entirely while spending much of her campaign time cultivating the minority vote.

Putting partisan politics aside, the Clinton campaign essentially threw many Old School values into the trash can in pursuit of progressive approval. This proved to be a fatal mistake at the ballot box.

A few examples. Defending the defenseless is a top-line Old School value. Even if you believe abortion is not immoral, allowing the destruction of a soon-to-be-born baby for a vaguely defined woman's "health" reason raises profound human rights questions.

Does it not?

Likewise, a permissive immigration policy goes against Old School orthodoxy. The open-borders situation in Europe is disastrous and dangerous, and the British recently rebelled against it by leaving the European Union.

And the presence of migrants is not really the driving force behind immigration control. No, it's the Old School doctrine of earning your way through life, and in the USA, that includes acquiring American citizenship legally. Giving that privilege away cheaply is not in the OS policy guide.

I could go on and on, but you get the idea. Under President Obama, many American traditions were attacked: the definition of marriage, the rights of religious people to follow their conscience, even the concept of justice as heinous hard drug dealers were suddenly defined as "nonviolent," despite the fact that they sell addictive poison that kills thousands of people every year.

Hillary Clinton bought into the Obama agenda totally.

So, many Old School folks had trouble supporting Mrs. Clinton, including those skeptical of Mr. Trump. Believe me, values were a major issue in the vote, even if they were overshadowed by economics. When you heard the appointment of Supreme Court justices mentioned by both candidates, that was all about values.

Had Secretary Clinton run as a traditionally minded liberal woman who basically respected Old School folks, she would be president today.

But by embracing the destructive agenda of the far left, she flunked out of Old School, and is now left to survey the wreckage that her disrespect for the OS curriculum wrought.

Five days before Election Day, I came to the conclusion that Hillary Clinton could lose. Few believed that. Here's the "Talking Points Memo" that I delivered on TV.

* * *

Hi, I'm Bill O'Reilly. Thanks for watching us tonight.

Congratulations to the Chicago Cubs. World Series champs.

Joe Maddon and his crew deserve it.

We'll talk about it in the "Tip of the Day."

But first . . . Hillary Clinton could lose the election.

That is the subject of this evening's "Talking Points Memo."

Most of the polls say the same thing. Donald Trump is gaining momentum.

FNC's analysis of the Electoral College now has Hillary Clinton only slightly above the 270 votes needed to win.

So, there should be grave concern in the Clinton camp.

The reason the secretary may lose the election is that the tipping point has been reached.

If you are familiar with Malcolm Gladwell's theory, bad things mount up, then suddenly, at a dramatic moment, everything comes crashing down.

For Hillary Clinton, the FBI may be the tipster.

Not only is the e-mail investigation reopened, but now Fox News is reporting that the Clinton Foundation is also under heavy scrutiny by federal investigators.

We will give you the facts on both stories in just a few moments.

It seems that many voters are becoming disenchanted with the whole Clinton situation because the controversies are endless.

We're not talking about fervent Democrats. Or liberal zealots.

We are talking about ordinary Americans who vote on the basis of what's best for the country.

Early in the campaign, "Talking Points" gave Hillary Clinton some good advice. And that was to speak directly to the American people through a series of interviews.

Explain the e-mail stuff.

Spell out the Clinton Foundation controversy.

Give straight answers to straight questions.

The Clinton campaign told us she would likely do an interview with the *Factor.*

That has turned out not to be true.

Even when Mrs. Clinton did appear here on the phone, talking about the terror attack in France, she indicated she was going to speak with me.

But this is not personal. Since September 12, Hillary Clinton has not done one national television interview with a journalist.

She is hiding.

She is also imperious, feeling that she is above questioning.

And if elected president, you can expect very little interaction with the press, or with the folks, from Hillary Clinton.

So, all of this—the continuing ethical problems, the detachment from the voters, the attitude that she deserves the presidency, all of it—is playing into her declining poll numbers.

There are five days left to the vote. We expect more hacking leaks. And perhaps some new personal attacks on Donald Trump.

But the only thing holding Mrs. Clinton up right now is Mr. Trump's negatives.

But they will not mean very much if the marginal Clinton support stays home on Election Day.

And that is a real possibility.

Summing up: Hillary Clinton thought she had this election

locked up. But she could very well find herself defeated come November 8.

The Tipping Point may have been reached.

And that's the memo.

* * *

Three days after that TV monologue, FBI chief James Comey announced that the Bureau's second look at the e-mail situation had not changed the equation: Hillary Clinton was not going to be charged with a crime.

The voters yawned.

It was all just too much. Secretary Clinton's résumé was loaded with one controversy after another, and her plan to create jobs was weak, to say the least. Essentially, she wanted to keep President Obama's political vision intact.

So, she was about as far away from Old School as a politician could get.

Change was in the air, and I knew it. Using Old School analysis, which never includes emotional deception, I told the world that Mrs. Clinton could lose.

I still believe that if Hillary Clinton had leveled with folks about her problems and what really motivated her in this life, she would have won. But she refused, trusting her political machine over sincere human interaction.

Not Old School.

So, the nation is now moving in a very different direction. Will that mean fostering OS values?

I'm praying.

Should we give Feirstein the last word on this?

* * *

Let's start by agreeing that no one is ever going to have the last word on the 2016 presidential election.

Whole forests are going to be felled for books about this. Coal mines will be reopened to power the Internet searches. Wind farms will sprout up across the land just to deal with the number of "What if?" and "If only" ruminations.

Little of it will explain what happened better than O'Reilly just did.

But as to his central question: Could Hillary Clinton have won the presidency if she'd pivoted to the center and addressed the nation in forthright, sincere speech, without focus testing and hedging every word?

Magic Eight Ball says, "Doubtful."

As my grandmother would have put it, "Sure. And if Hillary Clinton had wheels, she could have been a bus."

After thirty-plus years in the public eye, that just wasn't part of her political DNA.

That said, I'm not going to chew up pages here revisiting my views on the election. Instead, let's take this opportunity to announce a bold, fresh project:

Les Deplorables
The New Broadway Musical

In the tradition of *Hamilton*, and Victor Hugo's *Les Misérables*, we're pleased to present the epic story of America's 2016 presidential election, featuring:

Madam Secretary Clinton: *the presumptive nominee, who'll enter from stage left, with her rousing opening anthem, "It's My Turn."*

This will be followed by the rest of her campaign songbook:

"You Don't Know Me"
"Everybody Does the E-Mail Server"
"Somebody Rid Me of This Socialist"
"I'm So Entitled"
"What's My Message?"
"Let's Fall in Like"
"Pantsuits and Pandering"
"Basketful of Deplorables"
"It's Not Me, It's Misogyny"

After Madam Secretary's tragic loss at the polls, she'll sing her sorrowful, heartrending ballad, "Glass Ceilings," with its poignant lyrics:

The server in the basement, my lust for all that cash . . .
I just want you to note . . . I won the popular vote . . .
And I'll blame everyone else for my spectacular crash.

In the course of the evening, Mrs. Clinton will be reintroduced to the audience twenty-seven times.

Le Donald: *descending to the stage from a gold-plated Boeing 757, he will enter singing what will soon become his signature refrain:*

Enough with political correctness, enough with terrorists who hate . . .
Believe me when I tell you, I'm the one who can make America Great.

Later in the show, his other numbers will include:

"Build That Wall!"
"We're Havin' a Tweet Storm!"
"Extreme Vetting"
"A Little Locker Room Banter"
"Drain That Swamp"
and...
"The Ballad of Crooked Hillary"

At the end of the show, memberships at the No Longer Owned by Donald Trump Resorts and Golf Courses will be available for purchase in the lobby, along with Clinton Foundation T-shirts.

The Court Reporters: *a.k.a. the national press, who will all fall in line, marching onstage, singing in one voice:*

We're the mainstream media, we'll tell you what to think...
We'll coo and sigh over Hillary's grandchild, but it's Trump's campaign we must sink...
We'll ignore Hillary's scandals, we'll invoke the KKK...
That's our job, it's what we'll do, to save the USA.
We must demolish Trump!

The day after the election, the press will sing their mournful ballad, "We Who Have Learned Nothing":

We'll blame the Kremlin, and make up stories about Fake News. We'll stomp our boots on anyone, who doesn't share our views.

After the show, the preprinted special edition of *Newsweek*, "Madame President: Hillary Clinton's Historic Journey to the White House" will also be on sale in the lobby.

Les Deplorables: *the men and women of flyover country, who rise up in rebellion to stop Madam Clinton's coronation, singing:*

> The TV says we're racists, angry and sexist to the core . . .
> But we'll have our say, on Election Day . . .
> That's when we'll settle the score!

The production will also feature these outstanding players, and their soulful tunes:

La Donna Brazile: *"I've Got a Question"*

The FBI's James Comey: *"Unindictable You"*

Little Marco and Low-Energy Jeb: *"It Wasn't Supposed to Go Down Like This"*

Bernie Sanders: *who won't sing, but who will be stricken when he realizes that abolishing the Electoral College will mean that no presidential candidate will ever emerge from his home state of Vermont, or bother to campaign there again.*

In addition, we'll also hear from these important voices, singing their signature refrains:

Les Célébrités: *"Leavin' on a Jet Plane . . . a Very Private Jet Plane . . . or Maybe Not"*

The Snowflake Chorus: *"There's a Space for Us . . . Somewhere a Safe Space for Us"*

Plus . . .

The Big Dog: *Bill Clinton, who'll attempt to console his wife by singing this sad, haunting soliloquy:*

> Dear Hillary Rodham . . .
> I know of life, and loss, I surely feel your pain . . .
> But just remember, just one thing:
> When it came to money and votes,
> I was the one who made it rain.

Finally, to sum it all up (the election and the Snowflake meltdown that followed), here's our narrator, **O'Reilly, William J.:**

> When everyone gets a trophy, no one learns how to lose.
> But I can't sing, and I don't dance, so I'll just give you the news:
> When things go wrong in Old School, you rise with strength and
>   pluck.
> So, I'll leave you with the words of Edward R. Murrow—
> "Good night, and good luck."

16

Facing Facts

At this point, Feirstein and I have presented a fairly strong lesson plan emphasizing that Old School values will strengthen and simplify your life. I am convinced of this because I deal with Snowflakes every single day and understand that culture very well.

If you watch me on television, you know I usually win the debates. That's because I prepare myself with facts and avoid the evasive tactics that Snowflakes often use.

To the frost crew, it's always about deflecting to another matter. Nail the flakes on their failure to correctly define Islamic terrorism, and they immediately bring up Bush and the Iraq War.

Tell the flake-meisters that the collapse of the family makes it harder for black children to compete, and they trot out slavery as a catch-all excuse for dysfunction.

Finding solutions to vexing problems is the Old School way. Invalid comparisons and PC rhetoric is Snowflake territory.

Here's my best Snowflake story from the annals of *The O'Reilly Factor.*

After the terrorist attacks on September 11, 2001, I was angry. Scores of people in my Long Island neighborhood had been murdered by the al Qaeda savages. Their children went to school with my children. Heartbreaking doesn't even come close to describing the aftermath.

Then the Hollywood celebrities appeared, organizing a TV telethon to help families devastated by the attack. A good thing, right? I was asked to appear, and I did. Tens of millions of dollars were raised.

Months passed. I began hearing from families who needed help but were not receiving it. My staff called some of the charities involved, like the Red Cross and the United Way, who were supposed to have distributed the money. They were chaotic and could not explain why the donated funds were being held up.

So, Old School guy that I am, I reported the situation on the air and asked the celebrities involved in the telethon to put pressure on the charities to step up. I thought all these famous people would be as appalled as I was.

Uh, no.

The actor George Clooney took the lead in attacking me. Somehow, I was the problem for demanding accountability. How dare I? Didn't O'Reilly know that Mr. Clooney starred in *Ocean's 11*?

To me, it was easy. If you ask someone to donate money, as these famous people had, then you have a moral obligation to see that the money is honestly handled.

But in the Snowflake world in which George Clooney lives, the intent is all that matters. Forget about accountability, no room for that in Snowflakeville. So, Clooney and some others ripped me and refused to confront the incompetent charities.

After relentlessly pounding home my point, we finally got some of the money freed up for the families. But it was a nasty fight.

A few years later, I ran into Clooney and had a polite conversation with him. Old School people will attempt détente. But a couple of days later, Clooney hammered me again.

A Snowflake move.

My late mother, Angela O'Reilly, liked everybody. But even she thought Clooney was misguided and couldn't understand why some of her friends were siding with him.

I tried to explain to her that some folks have a sense of entitlement, that in their minds, they *never* do anything wrong, and if they're successful, they get away with it.

Sitting at her small kitchen table, my mom looked perplexed. So, I took her back in time.

"Mom, remember in sixth grade when I got suspended from school for punching Tommy Massey?

"How could I ever forget that? I thought your father would kill you."

"Do you recall what I said at the time?"

"I just remember you had an excuse."

"My excuse was that Tommy was an informant. He squealed to the teacher."

"Oh, you always had an excuse, Billy. Some of them were funny."

"Exactly, Mom. I never thought I deserved criticism because I was ten. That's what ten-year-olds do, make excuses for bad behavior. But George Clooney isn't ten. Arrested development, Ma, come on."

"Well, you certainly were a lively boy, Billy."

My mother then got up and cut me a piece of pie. Stale, but I ate it.

The point is that everyone makes mistakes, and people should admit to them. That's the Old School way. Face the facts. They are the lifeblood of the OS presentation.

I never should have punched Tommy Massey, and I deserved the punishment I received simply because I got away with a lot of other stuff. So, it was karma.

Snowflakes totally discount karma because they rarely do anything wrong. It's always Bush's fault or Trump's fault or O'Reilly's fault.

Just ask George Clooney.

The Old School Final Exam

We live in unsettled times.

Do you live your life with a growing sense of angst and anger, convinced of your own righteousness, attributing the worst of intentions to everyone who disagrees with you, believing the future is bleak, and hopeless?

Or do you get up in the morning with a sense of hope and promise, knowing there will always be struggles, but believing that, with hard work and humility and determination, preserving what worked in the past and embracing what is good in the present, one way or another, step by step, guided by common sense, we will all arrive at a better tomorrow?

We think you know the Old School answer.

17

Class Dismissed

Before Feirstein and I let you go, we'd like to give you a few more OS dictums to take with you. Just in case you get caught in a sudden snow shower or trapped in San Francisco:

— Old School grads do not hang with phonies. Insincerity to us is like a cross to a vampire.

— There should be signs that read, "Old School Zone: Fines for Speeding and Whining Will Be Doubled."

— Old School folks do not care about complaining housewives on TV, snarky political pundits who use "at the end of the day" in every other sentence, millionaire rappers who run down the police, pro football players who think Fidel Castro was a good guy, and global warming adherents whose own carbon footprint is bigger than Godzilla's. By the way, can't somebody put a solar panel on that giant beast?

— Old School people never swear in front of children, and they call out people who do.

— The OS code says if you see someone in distress, you try to help that person.

— Old School folks have a hard time paying five bucks for a latte, a scoop of ice cream, or a twenty-seven-ounce bottle of water from Fiji, where the local word for sucker is *sucker.*

— Old School leisure time does not usually include watching zombies snack on folks, punching up Internet sites that celebrate bad will, or sending your mom a birthday text instead of a nice card that cost a few bucks. Mom is no fool; she knows a diss when she sees one.

— And, by the way, if you do send cards for birthdays and Christmas, write a personal message on them. Just signing your name is lazy. Old School interactions should mean something.

— OS sensibility does not really embrace the LOL code. First off, chances are you did *not* laugh out loud at the text you received. The heavy odds are that text was completely meaningless, so why deceive? Instead, text back VB, for "very boring." Or, if you'd like to be more tactful, LST, "let's stop this!" Same thing with OMG! Do you think God likes seeing that every ten seconds? No, he does not! If you witness an alien spacecraft landing in your backyard, *then* you can say, "Oh, my God!" Until that time, leave the deity out of it.

— In general, Old School folks tend to be sentimental about kids, pets, old movies, the old neighborhood, and really funny people like Robin Williams, Jonathan Winters, Steve Martin, and Johnny Carson. Also, the OS crew admires veterans, teachers, honest public servants, and skilled performers onstage and on the field.

— But most of all, Old School folks admire friends who are loyal, generous, and honest. OS grads know these are very hard to come by.

In writing this book, we have tried to put forth why we believe the Old School philosophy works and is good for you personally and for the country. We hope you have enjoyed the ride.

It's important to note that we see the Snowflake opposition as more misguided than horrendous, although there are exceptions, as you well know.

Finally, we want to end with yet another Old School value: gratitude.

Thanks very much for reading our book.

The Snowflake Glossary

We use a lot of catchphrases and buzzwords in this book. So, to be totally clear—an Old School trait—here is a glossary, a cheat sheet, to put it all into perspective.

Snowflake. An exquisitely sensitive human being who is often more interested in feelings than facts. These people require constant protection from anything they find upsetting, anything that will cause them to experience feelings of fear, outrage and/or anger.

Social media. The catch-all description for Facebook, Twitter, Instagram, and Snapchat. A bit of a misnomer, given how much depraved, angry, and anti-social behavior they promote.

Social justice warrior. A politically active Snowflake who is committed to fighting all forms of oppression—especially if it means oppressing the views and voices of people they disagree with.

Ethnic or gender studies. What social justice warriors major in at college, where they learn about "root causes."

Root cause. The Snowflake's all-purpose phrase for avoiding blame, or taking personal responsibility for anything. So instead of arresting someone for throwing a rock through a window, we have to find the *root causes* for it—which usually lie somewhere in the way the corporate, colonialist, American patriarchy has been oppressing you for 250 years. Or something like that.

The patriarchy. White guys.

Diversity. People Snowflakes agree with.

Inclusion. More people Snowflakes agree with.

A dialogue. They talk, you listen.

A national dialogue. Same as in previous entry, but with microphones, TV cameras, and proposals for new laws, regulations, and government agencies designed to advance the Snowflake agenda. They legislate, you pay for it.

Cisgendered. A male who identifies as male, or a female who identifies as female. Derived from the Latin suffix *cis*, being the opposite of *trans*.

Heteronormative. The academic way of saying someone is ignorant, regressive, and probably still walks on his knuckles, because those who use the term believe heterosexuality is "normal."

Trigger warning. The heads-up that Snowflakes demand they be given before the utterance of anything that could possibly make them feel bad. The Snowflake equivalent of the MPAA warnings that appear in movie advertising. It's not entirely crazy to think they would have wanted someone to say, "Warning: the following may contain references to war, death, and slavery" before Lincoln got up to deliver the Gettysburg Address.

Safe space. Originally from the corporate world, a place where you could express any viewpoint or opinion without fear of repercussion. Now it's someplace that protects the Snowflakes from hearing any viewpoint or opinion other than what they want to hear.

Microaggression. Any seemingly innocent word or action that offends Snowflakes. Have you ever walked into a meeting and greeted the men and women at the table with the phrase "Hey, guys!"? You can't do that anymore. To Snowflakes, the word *guys* signals male dominance, and is a microaggression against all the women in the room

Dog whistle. Things that can only be heard by dogs—or, words and phrases with "secret, nefarious meanings" that can only be interpreted by talking heads on CNN.

Cultural appropriation. Taken to its logical end, your Irish mother really shouldn't be making Italian food.

Privilege. A neat piece of linguistic jujitsu employed by social justice warriors. You can't say you haven't benefited from privilege, because you're not even aware of your own privilege.

Racist. The first thing you call someone you disagree with.

Sexist. The second thing you call someone you disagree with.

Misogynist. The third thing you call someone you disagree with.

Fascist. The fourth thing you call someone you disagree with.

Hitler. When everything else fails, this is the insult of last resort. As they say on the Internet, sooner or later every argument devolves into someone calling someone else Hitler.

Illustration Credits

About the Authors

Bill O'Reilly is the anchor of *The O'Reilly Factor*, the highest-rated cable news show in the country. He is the author of many number-one bestselling books, including *A Bold Fresh Piece of Humanity*, *Culture Warrior*, and the hugely successful *Killing* series.

Bruce Feirstein is a screenwriter of the James Bond films *GoldenEye*, *Tomorrow Never Dies*, and *The World Is Not Enough* and the *New York Times* bestselling author of *Real Men Don't Eat Quiche*. He has written for *The New York Times* and *The Wall Street Journal* and has been a contributing editor at *Vanity Fair* since 1994.